P9-DIJ-597

Irma's SAMPLER

The Netherlands

Irma Eskes

That Patchwork Place®

Acknowledgments

I would like to thank the following people:

Nancy J. Martin, president of That Patchwork Place, for giving us the opportunity to become widely known through this book;

Barbara Weiland, editor-in-chief, for her thorough knowledge and guidance in making this book a success;

Brent Kane for his enthusiasm and expert photography;

My staff—Aad, Heleen, Marije, Yola, and Wil—for their never-ending support and creativity;

My husband, Cees, who worked so hard to help me reach my goals—a quilt shop of my own and now this book in the Quilt Shop Series;

All those who contributed their quilts for photography;

Marian Polak for telling us the history of the Dutch Quiltersgilde;

Liesbeth Ernst for her explanation of the traditional Dutch cotton fabrics;

Marije Maarsen for her tribute to the Peacock Quilters;

Peter Slabbers for my personal photo;

My friends who take so much interest in the weal and woe of my shop;

And to my customers, who have become my friends through the years.

THAT PATCHWORK PLACE MISSION STATEMENT

We are dedicated to providing quality products that encourage creativity and promote self-esteem in our customers and our employees.

We strive to make a difference in the lives we touch.

That Patchwork Place is an employee-owned, financially secure company.

Credits

Editor-in-Chief . . . . Barbara Weiland
Technical Editor . . . . Barbara Weiland
Managing Editor . . . . Greg Sharp
Copy Editor . . . . Liz McGehee
Proofreader . . . . Tina Cook
Design Director . . . . Judy Petry
Text Design . . . . Linda Trujillo
Typesetting . . . . Linda Trujillo
Photography . . . . Brent Kane
Illustration and Graphics . . . . Brian Metz
Translator . . . . Ineke van der Weele

No part of this product may be reproduced in any form, unless otherwise stated, in which case reproduction is limited to the use of the purchaser. The written instructions, photographs, designs, projects, and patterns are intended for the personal use of the retail purchaser and are under federal copyright laws; they are not to be reproduced by any electronic, mechanical, or other means, including informational storage or retrieval systems, for commercial use.

The information in this book is presented in good faith, but no warranty is given nor results guaranteed. Since That Patchwork Place, Inc., has no control over choice of materials or procedures, the company assumes no responsibility for the use of this information.

Irma's Sampler©
© 1994 by Irma Eskes
That Patchwork Place, Inc.
PO Box 118, Bothell, WA 98041-0118 USA

Printed in the United States

99 98 97 96 95 94   6 5 4 3 2 1

Library of Congress
Cataloging-in-Publication Data

Eskes, Irma,
Irma's Sampler / Irma Eskes.
   p. cm.—(International quilt shop series)
ISBN 1-56477-059-1 :
l. Irma's Sampler
(Shop : Haarlem, Netherlands)
2. Quilting—Patterns.
3. Patchwork—Patterns.
4. Quilts. I. Title. II. Series.
TT835.E83 1994   94-17056
746.9'7—dc20   CIP

Table of Contents

WELCOME TO IRMA'S SAMPLER   4

Classes and Workshops   5
Fabrics   5

A Little Bit of Haarlem   6
Special Quilts from Special People   7
   Necktie Quilt   7
   Scheveningen   8
   Map of the Netherlands   8
   Grow and Flourish   9
Dutch Village Fabrics   10
   A Little History   11
   Dutch Fabrics Today   12

THE QUILTS AND PROJECTS   13

   Orange Up!   14
   "Good Heavens"   18
   Crib Quilt   22
   Christa   25
   Dutch Bouquet   30
   Tempo Doeloe   34
   Reflexion   41
   Delft Blue   47
   Cow Quilt   49
   Reversible Quilt   55
   Feathers   58
   Red, White, and Blue   62
   Stars in Noord-Holland   66
   Stars in Holland   70
   Christmas Greeting Cards   74
   St. Nicolaas Doll Cookie   78

GENERAL DIRECTIONS   79

Fabric Selection for Patchwork
   and Appliqué   79
Quiltmaking Supplies   79
Patchwork Techniques   80
   Making and Using Templates   80
     Templates for Machine Piecing   80
     Templates for Hand Piecing   80
   Piecing   81
     Machine Piecing   81
     Hand Piecing   81
     Pressing   82
Appliqué   83
   Freezer-Paper Appliqué   83
   The Traditional Appliqué Stitch   83
   Borders   84
   Borders with Mitered Corners   84
   Borders with Straight-Cut Corners   85
Quilt Finishing   86
   Marking the Quilting Lines   86
   Layering the Quilt Sandwich   86
   Quilting   86
   Binding   86
   Making a Label   88

Irma Eskes, shop owner, Irma's Sampler

Welcome to Irma's Sampler

My adventure with quilting began ten years ago. As a teacher of textile arts, it was only natural that I tried my hand at quilting. I taught quiltmaking and sold the appropriate materials to my students. This experience, along with my own growing enthusiasm for quiltmaking, led me to open a shop that would better serve my students and others interested in patchwork and quilting. The result was Irma's Sampler, located in Haarlem, The Netherlands, about a fifteen-minute drive west from Amsterdam. I opened my shop in the fall of 1988, with my good friend Christa Mekenkamp. Unfortunately, Christa passed away last year. A quilt made in her memory appears on page 26.

I named my shop "Irma's Sampler" for several reasons. First of all, Irma is my given name. My personal relationship with my customers is very important to me. In addition, the "sampler" is a well-known item in patchwork and quilting, as well as in embroidery. Just as a sampler is a collection of different patterns and designs, my shop is a "sampler," providing a variety of fabrics, tools, and supplies. In the beginning, I offered materials for embroidery, silk painting, lace making, and origami, in addition to patchwork and quilting fabrics and supplies. Today, in addition to quiltmaking fabrics and supplies, you can still find lace-making supplies at Irma's Sampler. A beautiful lace peacock, the symbol of Irma's, appears in the photo at the bottom of page 5. It was made by Karin Nouwen, who teaches lace making at Irma's Sampler.

4

Classes and Workshops

At Irma's Sampler, we offer an extensive and varied class program each fall and spring, including the sampler quilt "Grow and Flourish" shown in the photo on page 9. Other popular classes include those on basic appliqué and machine piecing. Favorite quilt classes include Double Wedding Ring, Log Cabin, and Mariner's Compass. Celtic quilting is also popular.

The number of special classes and workshops I sponsor continues to increase. In addition, several internationally known teachers, including Nancy J. Martin, Mary Coyne Penders, Marsha McCloskey, and Jeana Kimball have taught workshops for our customers. It was an honor and a pleasure to have them visit my shop to teach us their exciting new methods.

Fabrics

Besides a wide range of fabrics from the United States, Japan, and Thailand, our own Dutch fabrics are quite popular for quiltmaking. Many of our homegrown fabrics are handwoven. For that reason, some are rather heavy and not suitable for patchwork and quilting. However, there are many good-quality Dutch fabrics in a weight that is appropriate for quiltmaking, and they are widely used! On this page and on pages 10–11, you will find samples of a variety of these colorful fabrics. A bit of history on Dutch fabrics begins on page 11. Many of the quilts made for this book feature typical Dutch fabrics, many of which I carry in my shop.

Traditional Dutch fabrics, counterclockwise: Woven stripe; "Sits"; Volendam Village floral; Volendam Village print; Volendam Village stripe for skirts; Woven stripes; Woven plaid; floral prints used for bed pillows and linens.

Karin Nouwen designed this lace pattern to imitate Irma's logo, the peacock. It is executed in #80 cotton thread. Karin also teaches lace making at Irma's.

A Little Bit of Haarlem

Haarlem, the lovely old Dutch city where Irma's Sampler is located, offers you a number of small enchantments—some of them one of a kind. Our town was granted municipal rights in 1245 and was built around the Grote Markt (Big Market). It has many famous buildings, including the Townhall, dating back to 1245; the Basiliek St. Bavo, built in 1470; and Vleeshal, built in 1603.

1. Corrie ten Boom Museum
2. Big Market
3. New Church
4. Old Chemist
5. Teylers Museum
6. Bakenes "Hofje"
7. Bakenes Church
8. Irma's Sampler/
   Frans Hals Museum

Irma's Sampler is a honey pot of supplies and ideas for quilters. When the renovation of the shop was completed and the doors first opened, Irma felt as proud as a peacock! The signboard reads: "Creativity in Craft."

The paving on Groot Heiligland is just as varied as the stone tablets on the building facades, indicating the trades of the occupants in the early days. Number 66 is Irma's Sampler, a treasure trove for all quilters. Our neighbor down the street is the Frans Hals museum. This magnificent building was originally a home for elderly men. It now harbors a permanent collection of seventeenth-century Dutch paintings.

Don't leave Haarlem without first enjoying a walk along the Spaarne River and visiting some of the eighteen "hofjes" (houses grouped around a garden or square, surrounded by a gate or a brick wall). Here you can live a very peaceful and secluded life. Of course, you will want to visit Amsterdam, just a short drive east, and don't miss the five working windmills in the village of Zaanse Schans.

Necktie Quilt by Winnie Vonk, 1990, Bennebroek, The Netherlands, 59" x 82". Hand pieced and hand quilted, Winnie's quilt (draped across the table) was made in loving memory of her husband, Henk. Standing, left to right: Wil Vuyk, Marije Weustink, Aad Kuenen, Yola van Ojen. Seated, left to right: Ineke van der Weele, Irma Eskes (shop owner), Heleen Aten.

Special Quilts from Special People

I would like to share with you several special quilts created by special people—my customers and my staff. Patterns are not given in this book for these quilts, but I thought you would like to see how creative and talented Dutch quilters are.

Necktie Quilt

In 1992, Winnie Vonk, one of my customers, celebrated her eightieth birthday. Just ten years earlier, after a visit to relatives in the United States and Canada, she had taken up quiltmaking. Ever since then, quiltmaking has been the focal point of her life. When Winnie lost her husband, she decided to donate his clothing to a charity project in Rumania. Although she did not know what she would do with them at the time, Winnie could not part with her husband's neckties. Before long, she realized why she had kept them. They would make a beautiful memory quilt. When she realized that she did not have enough neckties for her project, she asked relatives and neighbors to contribute, which they did with love.

When the quilt was completed, Winnie took it with her to the annual quilt show of the Dutch Quiltersgilde in Naarden. While she was quilting, show visitors stopped to see her delightful quilting stitches. When men passed by, they carefully held their neckties, afraid that Winnie might cut them off for her next quilt. As a result of that Sunday spent quilting in public, she received dozens of neckties from all over the country. Who knows? Perhaps one day, we will see another of Winnie's wonderful necktie quilts.

Scheveningen by Wil Vuyk, 1992, Alphen ald Rijn, The Netherlands, 37" x 37". This quilt was made from fabrics from Scheveningen costumes—jackets, caps, and aprons.

Scheveningen

BY WIL VUYK

This quilt is a tribute to my Scheveningen background. Scheveningen is a town in the southwestern part of the Netherlands, on the North Sea. The idea came to me while I was attending the opening ceremony of Quilt Expo 1992 in The Hague, during the performance of the Scheveningen Fish Wives Choir.

The fabrics in this quilt came from special people. My mother gave me a bag of scraps, including an old apron that I used in the outer border. I also used fabrics from my grandmother's Scheveningen cap. One of the women in the choir gave me some of the fabrics that are used in the Scheveningen costumes today, and the white selvages in the black border were cut from an old apron. In the early days, these white edges were woven into the fabric. Nowadays, the women sew a white ribbon onto the edge of new fabric in imitation of the old. The gray woolen fabric scraps came from my grandpa's jacket, and the striped fabric is from my father's wedding costume, now nearly sixty years old. The ribbon at the bottom of the quilt was used to protect skirt seams against wear and tear. It is called *bezemband* (bezem=broom). The quilting pattern, three crowned herrings, is based on the armorial of Scheveningen.

Map of the Netherlands

BY THE PEACOCK QUILTERS

One day, some months after I opened my quilt shop, Christa and I decided to start a quilt group. Besides running the quilt shop, we wanted to be actively involved in quilting. We invited some quilters from Haarlem and the surrounding area to attend the first meeting at the shop. Everyone was asked to bring something for "Show and Tell." After that first gathering, we agreed to work together on various projects that would promote quilting. Our first project was a patchwork quilt for children, featuring easy-to-recognize, everyday objects. We donated the finished quilt to a school for handicapped children.

Over the years, we have continued to meet at Irma's Sampler and to visit quilt shows and participate in quilting workshops. We often had very serious discussions about what to call ourselves. One day I received a letter addressed to "The Peacock's," probably because there is a peacock on the store signboard. We came to the unanimous decision that "Peacock Quilters" it should be!

In April 1992, when our country hosted "Quilt Expo Europa III," the Dutch Quiltersgilde held their annual quilt show. Members were asked to contribute quilts featuring the Netherlands. To meet the chal-

Nederland by Hoog en by Laag by the Peacock Quilters, 1992, Haarlem, The Netherlands, 59" x 69". This group quilt was made of several kinds of fabrics, including rayon, cotton, and silk. It was machine pieced and hand quilted by the group members.

Grow and Flourish by Kea Gutker de Geus-Ploegman, 1992, Wijdenes, The Netherlands, 43" x 47". Popular classes at Irma's Sampler include this sampler quilt taught by Heleen Aten.

lenge, we set out to design a quilt for our group, based on the topographical colors used on the reference map of an atlas of the Netherlands.

On the full-scale drawing, radii and circles were drawn with Haarlem as the center. Green and violet were the colors for land, blue for the sea, and neutrals for the neighboring countries. We all turned our scrap bags upside down and after a lot of grabbing, we each went home with countless scraps of cotton, rayon, silk, and polyester satin in a great variety of tints and shades of green, violet, and blue to make our assigned segment of the map. With a bit of juggling, we managed to fit the pieces together. We machine pieced the quilt, using a little appliqué here and there. Everyone helped with the hand quilting. This complex project promoted friendship and lots of laughter. Best of all, perhaps, the finished quilt was exhibited at The Hague and has appeared on the June 1992 cover of *Quiltnieuws*, the colorful quarterly magazine published by the Dutch Quiltersgilde.

Members of the Peacock Quilters include: Heleen Aten, Irma Eskes, Gerda Groeneveld, Norita Ingenhoust, Aad Kuenen, Marije Maarsen, Marian Polak, Tine Veerman, and Coby Verkuylen (and Christa Mekenkamp, now deceased).

Grow and Flourish
BY KEA GUTKER DE GEUS-PLOEGMAN

This quilt is the result of an inspiring quilt class taught by Heleen Aten, a well-known teacher at Irma's Sampler. When I finished this quilt, I named it "Grow and Flourish" because all the blocks are related to that theme.

Blocks include:

1. The traditional Drunkard's Path in the center, reaching out to the other blocks. The quilted fleur-de-lis represents "the flame of light, life and power."
2. Bulbs and tulips, representing growth from bulb to bloom
3. The logo of the Dutch Quiltersgilde
4. Flower and leaf motifs in trapunto, with appliquéd doves of peace
5. Buckeye blossoms (appliqué)
6. Tangerine (appliqué)
7. Flower in full bloom
8. Heart medallion frame from *Baltimore Beauties and Beyond* by Elly Sienkiewicz. Quilted hearts repeat the theme.
9. Ringed Star, in honor of Irma and Christa, the founders of Irma's Sampler. I finished my sampler with this block because the ring is the symbol of eternal love.

Dutch Village Fabrics

Hans Brinker, the brave little boy who used his finger to prevent a break in the dike that protects the region against floods, became the symbol of the perpetual struggle of the Netherlands against the sea. In 1865, the well-known American author Mary Mapes Dodge wrote *Hans Brinker or The Silver Skates*. The film version of this book shows the principal characters in Volendam costumes, often regarded as "the real Dutch costume."

Although Hans Brinker was a fictional character, the costumes are real. Even today, these clothes are worn by people of Volendam, a small community near the former Zuider Zee. When visiting the village and the harbor, you will see women in their black-and-gray striped jackets with intricate ruffles. Underneath their black skirts, they wear a brightly colored, striped underskirt. Over these they wear an apron made of a neatly starched, very colorful striped fabric, the so-called "Volendammer Streep."

A three-string coral necklace with a golden snap is an important part of the attire, along with the *hull*, a cap with upright wings made of lace. In addition to the necklace, women wear a loosely tied crocheted *dasje* of blue and white, bordered with tassels.

The men of Volendam, mostly the sailors and fishermen, wear a striped shirt, large, wide trousers, and a black jacket made of heavy woolen material adorned with silver buttons.

Volendam is not the only region where costume wearing has prevailed. The nearby fishing village of Marken, once an island, is now attached to the mainland by a dike. Houses here are still furnished according to the old tradition. You'll also find traditional costumes in Bunschoten-Spakenburg, as well as in Staphorst, with its handsomely renovated farmhouses painted in bright blue and green. Although less well known than the costumes of Volendam, these costumes are special and sometimes are even more colorful.

Today, traditional Dutch cotton fabrics originate from the costumes and from the villages just mentioned, where they are also used in home furnishings. You can still buy traditional fabrics in small shops in Volendam, Marken, Spakenburg, and Staphorst.

Dutch costumes are bound to certain areas and regions and are barely influenced by the contemporary fashion cycles. This is due to the geographical situation, the rules within religious communities, and the traditions within certain groups, such as farmers and fishermen. Each village and each region has its own social rules and its own ways of using fabric and color in clothing and in furnishings. Some garments, patterns, and colors used in costumes date as far back as the seventeenth century. In Marken, Volendam, Staphorst, and in other areas where regional costumes are still worn, you will see them especially on market days and at church, when villagers parade in their well-

Mrs. Visser, dressed in the traditional costume of Marken, is a familiar face in the local fabric store, where you can buy traditional Dutch Village fabrics. In the background, Stars in Noord-Holland by Akka Philips sparkles in the sun. For quilt directions, see page 66.

10

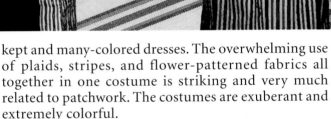

kept and many-colored dresses. The overwhelming use of plaids, stripes, and flower-patterned fabrics all together in one costume is striking and very much related to patchwork. The costumes are exuberant and extremely colorful.

Costume wearing is a serious matter. Every detail has a subtle meaning. If you are in the know, you can learn a lot about the life, the social status, the age, and the origin of the wearer by examining the details of the costume. For example, you can tell at first glance whether a person is a girl or a young woman or whether she is engaged or recently married. You can also identify a widow, who can use her costume to reveal that she will consider a new marriage. Fisherman, tenant, or landlord—these occupations are also distinguished by subtleties in dress. In addition, certain details reveal whether someone belongs to the Protestant or to the Catholic Church.

Little children, up to the age of five, until recently wore skirts. Certain details in the garment and the way in which the fabrics were used revealed whether the child was a boy or a girl.

Just as black symbolizes mourning in many cultures, Dutch costume reflects this emotional state too. There are three degrees of mourning: deep mourning, half mourning, and light mourning. In addition to black fabrics, lilac-and-white, lilac-and-black, violet, deep violet, and a wide variety of blue fabrics are used for Dutch mourning costumes. These fabrics may even be pretty flower prints. However sad it may be to lose a loved one, life goes on!

A Little History

In the early days of our country, clothes were made primarily from wool and linen. The raw material was readily available. Wool came from the sheep; linen came from flax plants. Plants, animals, and fruit provided the raw material for fabric dyes as well as the inspiration for the designs. Fabrics were hand dyed or printed with stamp blocks. For embellishment, intricate patterns were knit, embroidered, or woven into the fabrics. Because the techniques used were so time-consuming, these sumptuous fabrics were very expensive. Moreover, they were heavy to wear and not easily laundered.

After the formation of the V. O. C. (Dutch East Indies Company) in the beginning of the seventeenth century, Indian chintzes came into use in Holland. They were favored for their deep colors and beautiful designs. These fabrics were hand painted, smooth, shiny, washable, colorfast, and above all, comparatively inexpensive. The large pieces of chintz went to the rich. Whoever could lay their hands on a small piece of this very special fabric was as happy as a king. Women used these tiny pieces of chintz in their costumes. Sometimes they were used as set-in pieces in place of the usual embroidered parts. To show off the riot of colors to best advantage, these fabrics were worn as collars and caps, or they were worn to cover the neck and shoulders, making the attire even more flattering.

The ships of the V. O. C. also brought home beautifully woven checkered fabrics, and cottons in an exceptional deep indigo blue with white printed flowers. The dye recipe was an Indian secret. These fabrics were used again and again as costumes were remade and altered. Even today, a Dutch woman cherishes an old piece of chintz. The Dutch are very thrifty when it comes to preserving their old fabrics!

The V. O. C. ships took a long time to sail home with their precious fabric cargo—sometimes as long as eighteen months. Because washable, colorful fabrics were in such demand, it seemed quite natural that the Dutch tried to copy these fabrics. By the end of the seventeenth century, the cotton industry was established in the west part of Holland. At first, they used cottons imported from India and engaged the help of Indian dye experts. Some of these fabrics were block printed; others were hand painted with colorful designs of high quality.

Colors such as deep red, lilac, violet, and deep violet were combined with black and white in some fabrics. Blue-and-white resist prints were very popular. To create them, the shapes of the flowers were printed on the cotton with a preserving paste that blocked the dye when immersed in an indigo dye bath.

Dutch Fabrics Today

Red, white, and blue in a wide range of shades and tints are still predominant in Dutch fabrics. These colors are common in our farmers' hankies, probably the most used piece of fabric in our climate. And, of course, our flag is red, white, and blue.

Dutch fabrics are not only characterized by color and design but also by the unlimited variety of bold stripes and plaids. Thanks to the costume wearing and the home furnishing style in these regions, traditional Dutch fabrics have remained in demand throughout the years. The Dutch cotton industry has continued to print and weave traditional fabrics. In Staphorst and Volendam, women print or paint fabrics that are needed in their costumes.

Besides beautiful dress materials, there are also dark striped fabrics for men's shirts and neckerchiefs, and plaids and flower prints for aprons and shawls for everyday use or as collectors' items.

Traditional cotton fabrics are used in dressmaking as well as in interior decorating. In the past, even costly chintzes and blue prints were used for these purposes. An exception to the rule are the cottons used for bedding—sheets, curtains for the cupboard beds, and pillowcases. The early cotton prints were rose, red, and black; nowadays they are rose and red on a white background. In periods of mourning, even the color of the bedding changes to lilac or blue with naive and graceful rose buds, roses in full bloom, feathers, cherries, and carnations.

Some people consider these fabrics rather boring because of their simple color schemes. For everyday use, they are, in fact, lovely, especially with the lacelike background. Moreover, they are inexpensive. If you

Blue-and-white resist print   *Hand-painted print from Staphorst*

are not too keen on flowers, there is also a rich choice of plaids and stripes for bedding, especially for bolster cases and ticking.

Are these fabrics still for sale? If you know the way, you can find many of these fabrics in the Netherlands. Chintzes and blue prints are reproduced on a small scale. There are also machine-printed blue-and-white fabrics that are similar to the antique blue prints. Furthermore, there are stripes and plaids used in working clothes, flower prints for aprons, many-colored stripes for underskirts and sleeves (as seen in Volendam and Marken), and fabrics with "farm roses," carnations, and small pear-shaped designs. There is also a unique collection of woven fabrics. Shawls in red or blue checks and flowers, fabrics for sheets, pillowcases, and ticking in typical stripes and checks are still available. In addition, you can often find beautiful fabrics imported from Austria, Switzerland, Germany, and France, but they have to meet the Dutch rules of tradition.

Thanks to our costumes and the ingenuity and thrift of the women who wear them, these fabrics were saved. It is a most impressive thing that even fabrics, however simple they may be, belong to the cultural heritage of a country. And it is wonderful to see them being used successfully in wonderful patchwork and appliqué quilts that express one of the characteristics of our country.

The Quiltersgilde of the Netherlands

The seed for quiltmaking was sown in the Netherlands by the traveling exhibition of antique quilts from the Jonathan Holstein collection in 1974, and by Sophie Campbell, an American who had been teaching quiltmaking in Paris. Almost ten years later, in the summer of 1983, twenty-one Dutch women met to start the Dutch Quiltersgilde. They had no idea that it would blossom into a group of over 8,000 members within the next ten years. Before founding the guild, they had been working in small groups with a teacher, or on their own at home, following directions in an American book on quilting. They kept in touch through a typewritten newsletter. Quilt shops did not yet exist, so supplies were difficult to find. They bought their fabrics on trips to the United States or at (dress) fabric stores in the Netherlands and other countries in Europe. They often swapped fabrics back and forth among themselves.

In the first year the guild existed, members started a tradition that has continued ever since. Each year, the guild sponsors an exhibit of members' work, holding it in a different location each year. In 1992, 13,000 visitors came to see the quilts at an eighteenth century church in The Hague!

The quilt show is not juried—a member may send any work that has not yet hung in a major exhibit. Regional groups (twenty-one of them) stage additional smaller shows during the year. They also hold meetings for local members twice a year so that people can keep in touch and exchange ideas and knowledge.

Every year, the Quiltersgilde organizes two week-long outings for quilters at a rural retreat. Several teachers present workshops and/or lectures for quilters of all skill levels. These "mini-vacations" are always a great success and those who attend love the opportunity to share the quiltmaking experience.

Membership in the Quiltersgilde is still growing. All work, including producing a beautiful quarterly publication, is done by volunteers. More teachers, a greater variety of workshops, and many quilt shops and books on quilting in the Dutch language have made quilting a popular hobby. Recently, many quilters have started using the Dutch traditional fabrics in their quilts, and many people are experimenting with new styles and techniques. Original work is emerging in a country that has had a tradition of quiltmaking since the seventeenth century, but that is quite another story.

The Quilts and Projects

In this section, you will find directions for wonderful quilts and projects that are typical of the ones Dutch quilters like to make. My staff and customers have willingly shared their work for this book. Most of the quilts feature typical Dutch fabrics, but you will find some American and European fabrics mixed in.

Dutch quilters still use traditional hand piecing and quilting methods (although they are learning to use rotary-cutting and strip-piecing methods too). For that reason, full-size templates are given for those quilts that require them. These templates include the necessary ¼"-wide seam allowances. If you prefer rotary-cutting methods, you may be able to cut many of the shapes by simply measuring and cutting them from fabric strips of the correct width.

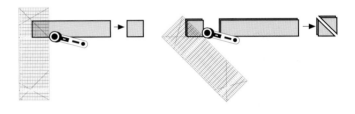

I hope you have enjoyed learning about quilting in the Netherlands and that you will enjoy making many of the colorful quilts in this book. We would love to see you in our shop in Haarlem if your travels bring you to the Netherlands.

Irma Eskes

Editor's Note: It was my distinct pleasure to travel to Haarlem with our staff photographer to do much of the photography featured in this book. Irma and her husband, Cees, and the staff at Irma's Sampler extended their warm Dutch hospitality, welcoming us to their light-filled shop and showing us their beautiful country. The visit was much too short! Thank you, Irma and Cees!

Orange Up!

ORANJE BOVEN!

BY MARIJE WEUSTINK-HUIJG

FINISHED SIZE: 60½" x 100½"
BLOCK SIZE: 10" x 10"

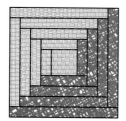

Log Cabin Block

*W*hen Irma asked me to design a quilt using typical Dutch fabrics, I accepted the challenge. I chose a Dutch theme, too, and made my quilt to represent our tricolor flag, adding an orange streamer for the queen. (See the history of our flag on page 17 for more information.) The orange streamer has inspired our sportsmen lately. At international championships, Dutch supporters wear orange—orange pants, jackets, socks, scarves, caps, etc. They make a colorful and striking show in a stadium.

This quilt was machine pieced, Log Cabin–style, on muslin foundations.

MATERIALS: 44"-WIDE FABRIC

¾ yd. orange
1½ yds. dark red
⅔ yd. light red
⅔ yd. white
⅔ yd. light blue
¾ yd. medium blue
1¼ yds. dark blue
5½ yds. muslin* for the block foundations
4 yds. for backing
62" x 102" piece of batting

*If your muslin is less than 44" wide after preshrinking, you will need an additional yard of muslin.

*Orange Up! by Marije Weustink-Huijg, 1993,
Haarlem, The Netherlands, 61" x 101". This bed quilt is
an original design Marije made for her son Thijs.*

Cutting

It is easiest to cut and assemble only one set of blocks at a time. Make all the orange blocks (A) first, then the orange/red blocks (B), and so on, until you have cut and assembled all 60 blocks.

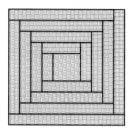

Block A
Orange
Make 6.

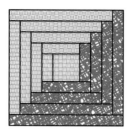

Block B
Orange/Dark Red
Make 4.

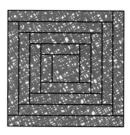

Block C
Dark Red
Make 11.

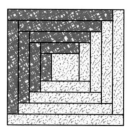

Block D
Dark Red/Light Red
Make 6.

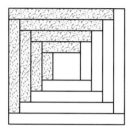

Block E
Light Red/White
Make 6.

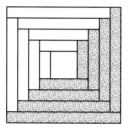

Block F
White/Light Blue
Make 6.

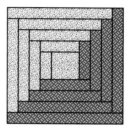

Block G
Light Blue/Dark Blue
Make 6.

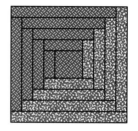

Block H
Dark Blue/Medium Blue
Make 9.

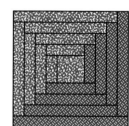

Block I
Medium Blue/Dark Blue
Make 6.

1. For each block, cut a 2½" x 2½" center square from the predominant color in the block. Refer to the quilt photo on page 15.
2. Cut 1½"-wide strips for the logs, cutting the strips across the fabric width.
3. From the muslin, cut 60 squares, each 11" x 11".

Directions

1. On graph paper, draft a full-size block, following the block diagram. Although it will measure 10½" square, it will finish to 10". Number each log as shown. The center square is 2½" wide and each log is 1" wide.
2. Using your drawing as a pattern underneath each block, use a pencil to trace the lines onto each 11" muslin square. Number each log position. Then complete each block, following steps 3–6.

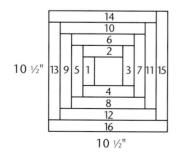

3. Place a center square of fabric, right side up, in the center square position. Pin or baste in place.

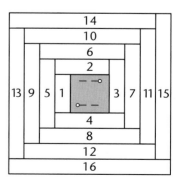

Pin center square in place on the marked foundation.

16

The Dutch Flag

In 1937 by royal decree, Queen Wilhelmina, Princess of Oranje Nassau, made red, white, and blue the official colors of the Dutch flag. However, the Dutch flag existed long before the royal decree made it official. Around the world, this color combination is perceived as a symbol of liberty and independence. Perhaps the Dutch flag served as an example for other national flags.

In 1568, the Dutch were involved in a war of independence against the mighty empire of Spain. They fought under the command of the Prince of Oranje Nassau. The color of the principality was Nassau blue, and these freedom fighters chose the orange, white, and blue flag as their symbol. Today, we still hang out an orange streamer on the birthdays of the Royal Family members, even though orange is no longer a color in our flag.

This war of independence lasted eighty years, and during that time, the colors of the flag gradually changed to red, white, and blue. The Dutch flag gained worldwide recognition as the Dutch dislodged the Spaniards from the Netherlands and conquered many Spanish settlements in North America, Africa, and Asia.

We proudly raise our flag on April 30, the official birthday celebration of our queen; May 4, Remembrance Day, when we commemorate all those who gave their lives in World War II; May 5, Liberation Day; and all days of the year when there is something special to celebrate, including weddings and anniversaries.

5. Continue stitching logs to the foundation square in the same manner, adding them in numerical order until the block is complete. Refer to each block diagram on page 16 for the correct color placement in each block. When completed, the muslin foundation should extend beyond the outer edges of the block.

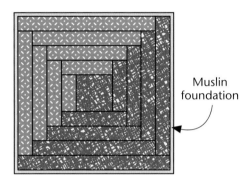

Muslin foundation

6. Trim the completed blocks to 10½" x 10½", cutting away the excess muslin.

Quilt Top Assembly

1. Arrange the completed blocks in 10 rows of 6 blocks each. Refer to the quilt photo on page 15 for color placement.
2. Sew the blocks together in horizontal rows, pressing the joining seams in opposite directions from row to row to make matching easier.
3. Sew the rows together to complete the quilt top.

Quilt Finishing

Refer to the general directions for quilt finishing, beginning on page 86.
1. Layer the quilt with batting and backing; baste.
2. Quilt in-the-ditch around all center squares. Quilt between the third and fourth log in the upper right corner and lower left corner of each block.
3. Piece the binding in appropriate lengths to match the block colors around the quilt; bind the quilt.

4. Lay a strip of the appropriate color for Log 1 face down on top of the center square. Line up the raw edge of the fabric with the inner line for Log 1 on the muslin. Stitch ¼" from the raw edge. Press the strip onto the muslin foundation. Trim the excess strip even with the inner line for Log 2.

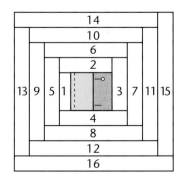

Sew first strip right side down onto center square.

"Good Heavens"

"Hemeltje lief"

BY AAD KUENEN

FINISHED SIZE: 18" x 28"

I am the fortunate heir to all of the dolls that belonged to my two grandmothers, so I have more than just the standard beds in my home to cover with quilts. That is why I chose to make this doll quilt. My inspiration for the design came from a Milky Way quilt from Whitlock, Tennessee, dated 1870. The dark fabric I used in this quilt is from Spakenburg. People who live in that area wear this specific fabric when they are in mourning. The lilac-colored fabric is also from Spakenburg and is used to make bedclothes.

The position of the lights and darks creates interesting effects in the two halves of this quilt. The larger, light hexagons seem to have a halo of six light pineapples, whereas the bigger, dark hexagons appear as the background for an intricate six-pointed star made of Log Cabin strips.

Materials: 44"-WIDE FABRIC

Because this quilt is so small, the materials requirements are given in total inches. Cut fabric strips across the fabric width (selvage to selvage).

5 different dark prints totaling 14" for the quilt center
5 different light prints totaling 14" for the quilt center
4" x 42" strip in medium tone for small center hexagons
4" x 42" strip in contrasting tone for inner border
4" x 42" light strip for middle border
12" x 42" dark strip for outer border and binding
20" x 28" piece of backing
20" x 28" piece of batting

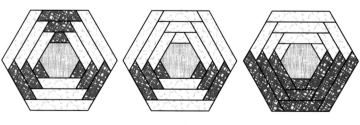

Block A
Make 7.

Block B
Make 8.

Block C
Make 2.

*"Good Heavens" ("Hemeltje Lief") by Aad Kuenen, 1993, Haarlem, The
Netherlands, 18" x 28". In the two halves of this little quilt, lights and darks reverse.
The larger light hexagons seem to have a nimbus of six light pineapples. The large
dark hexagons form the background for intricate six-pointed stars
made Log-Cabin style.*

Directions

Blocks

Use the templates on page 21. The quilt consists of 32 hexagons made Log Cabin style.

1. Using the full-size pattern below, trace 32 hexagons onto foundation paper. Cut out each one, leaving a 1"-wide allowance all around.

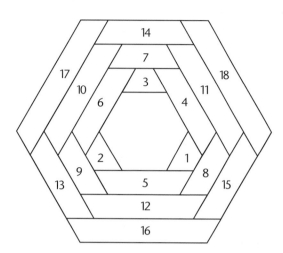

2. Trace Templates I and II onto plastic template material. Cut the templates from the plastic. Carefully cut out the triangle in the center of Template I and make a tiny hole at each seam intersection as indicated by the dots.

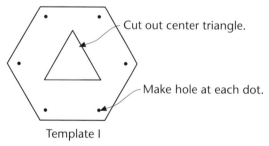

Template I

3. Using Template I, cut 5 dark and 5 light hexagons. Use a sharp pencil to mark the dots on the wrong side of each fabric hexagon.
4. Using Template II, cut 32 hexagons from the medium-tone strip.
5. Cut the remainder of the light and dark fabrics for the blocks into ¾"-wide strips.
6. Using the paper-foundation piecing method described on page 21, make the required number of hexagon blocks in each of the three required color arrangements. Refer to block diagrams on page 18.
7. Press each completed hexagon block lightly. Position Template I on each one, using the center triangle to guide the placement. Trim block even with the edges of the template. Mark the corner dots with a sharp pencil on the wrong side of each hexagon.

Quilt Top Assembly

1. Lay out the completed blocks, using the quilt plan on page 18 as a guide. Sew the blocks together, matching the dots and beginning and ending each seam at the corner dots.

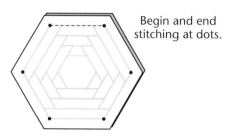

Begin and end stitching at dots.

2. Trim the blocks along the outer edges to create a rectangle.

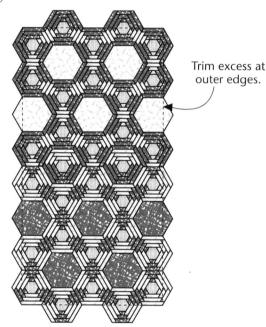

Trim excess at outer edges.

Borders

From the contrasting fabric for the inner border, cut:
    3 strips, each ¾" wide
From the light fabric for the middle border, cut:
    3 strips, each 1¼" wide
From the dark fabric for the outer border, cut:
    3 strips, each 3" wide

1. Sew each set of border strips together. Cut one set in half to use for the top and bottom borders.

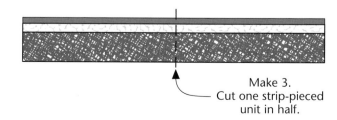

Make 3.
Cut one strip-pieced unit in half.

2. Sew the borders to the quilt, following the directions for "Borders with Mitered Corners" on pages 84–85.

Quilt Finishing

Refer to the general directions for quilt finishing, beginning on page 86.

1. Layer the quilt top with batting and backing; baste.
2. Quilt as desired. Use the border pattern provided on pullout pattern or another design of your choice.
3. Bind the edges with strips cut from the outer border fabric.

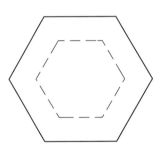

Good Heavens
Template II

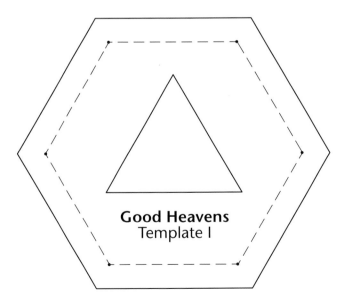

Good Heavens
Template I

Paper-Foundation Piecing

Block A is shown in the illustrations. Change the color of the strips as required for each different block coloration.

To make each hexagon:

1. Position a small hexagon right side up in the center of the paper foundation, matching seam lines and keeping raw edges even with the next set of stitching lines. Pin or baste in place.

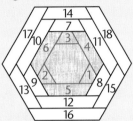

2. Place a ¾"-wide strip face down on the center hexagon as shown, extending one end beyond the edge of the center hexagon and keeping the long raw edge even with the hexagon's edge. Stitch ¼" from raw edges.

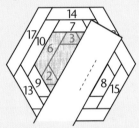

3. Press the strip toward the paper foundation. Cut the excess strip even with the edge of the center hexagon.

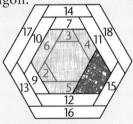

4. Continue adding strips of the appropriate color in the numerical order indicated until the block is completed.

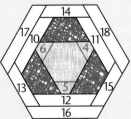

5. Carefully tear away the paper foundation from the completed block

Crib Quilt

WIDZE TEKKEN FOAR IN LYTSE POPPE

BY INEKE VAN DER WEELE

FINISHED SIZE: 38½" x 48½"
BLOCK SIZE: 5" x 5"

Make 48.

During the summer of 1992, I visited a show of antique Dutch quilts. I had not realized that Dutch women made so many quilts in the eighteenth century. I was delighted with a Friesian quilt, simply made from one regular shape—the right-angle triangle. In my quilt, I have tried to capture the charm of that old quilt with typical Dutch printed fabrics from different parts of the Netherlands. Some are old, some are new, and most are red or blue with a touch of yellow. If you look closely, you are sure to recognize some American checked fabrics as well. I hope that one day a happy grandchild will dream under this Dutch quilt.

Materials: 44"-WIDE FABRIC

Assorted scraps of blue, red, and yellow prints, varying in size from 6½" squares to 6½" x 44" strips (approximately 2 yds. of fabric)

3 yds. red print for border and backing

5" x 42" strip of blue solid for binding

42" x 52" piece of batting

Crib Quilt (Widze tekken foar in lytse poppe) by Ineke van der Weele, 1993, Maassluis, The Netherlands, 38½" x 48½". Photographed in the fishing village of Marken, the inspiration for this quilt came from an eighteenth-century Friesian crib quilt.

Directions

Blocks

1. Cut 96 triangles from the assorted scraps, using the template on page 24.

Cut 96.

2. Lay out the triangles in the desired finished arrangement, referring to the quilt plan on page 22.

3. Join each pair of triangles, right sides together, to form a half-square triangle unit. Press the seam to one side.

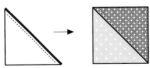

4. Join each set of 4 half-square triangle units to create a block. Make 12 blocks.

Make 12.

5. Join the blocks into rows of 3 blocks each, pressing the joining seams in opposite directions from row to row.

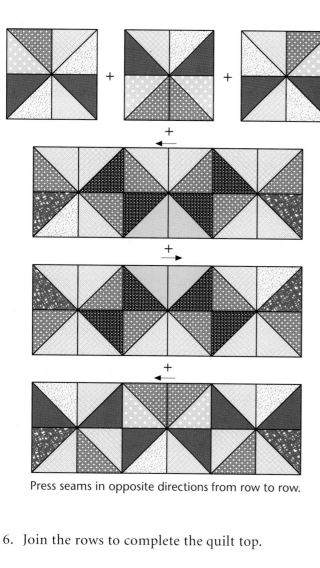

Press seams in opposite directions from row to row.

6. Join the rows to complete the quilt top.

Borders

Refer to "Borders with Mitered Corners," beginning on page 84.

1. Measure the quilt for borders with mitered corners. Cut 4½"-wide strips of the appropriate lengths, from the length of the fabric. Set the remaining fabric aside for the backing.
2. Sew the borders to the quilt top, mitering corners.

Quilt Finishing

Refer to the general directions for quilt finishing, beginning on page 86.

1. Layer the quilt top with batting and backing; baste.
2. Quilt. You may wish to outline quilt each triangle or quilt in-the-ditch. Quilt the borders in a pattern of your choice.
3. Bind the edges of the quilt with 1"-wide strips cut from the blue solid fabric.

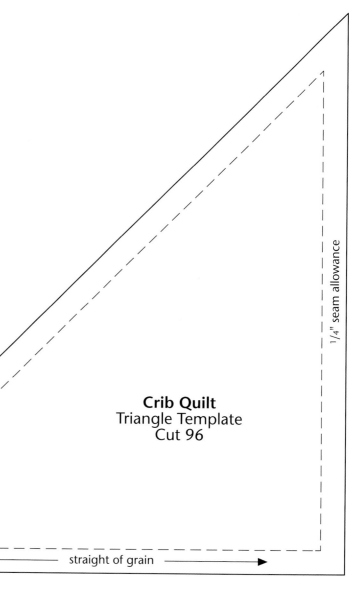

¼" seam allowance

Crib Quilt
Triangle Template
Cut 96

straight of grain

Christa

BY CATHERINE HESSELINK

FINISHED SIZE: 36½" x 36½"
BLOCK SIZE: 12" x 12"

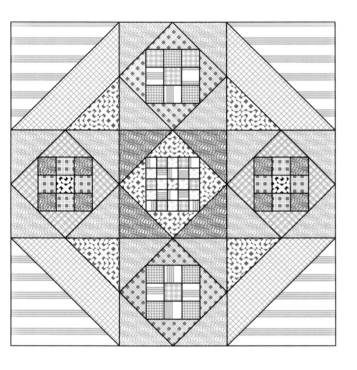

I made this quilt to reflect my interest in folk art, our national costumes, and the decorative arts used to embellish textiles for clothing and home decorating. Dutch fabrics in this quilt include bed ticking, kitchen curtains, red farmers' hankies, and black apron prints. In some places, the wrong side of the black prints was used for a muted gray effect. I made the back of the quilt from four farmers' hankies, three matching and one a so-called "empty hanky" with a Ninepatch block appliquéd in the center in homage of Christa Mekenkamp. She advised me to keep it in the quilt even though it didn't fit with the other blocks. Directions are not given for the backing, but you can create your own interesting pieced backing using hankies and scraps.

Materials: 44"-WIDE FABRIC

Scraps of assorted red prints, checks, and stripes in
    light, medium, and dark tones for the blocks
½ yd. total of assorted black prints for the blocks
⅓ yd. red-and-white ticking for outer block corners
¼ yd. red-and-white checked fabric for binding
1⅛ yds. for backing
41" x 41" piece of batting

Cutting

Use the templates on pages 28–29.

From light red fabrics, cut:
    25 Template A
    36 Template B

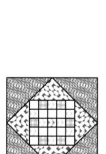

Block 1
Make 1.

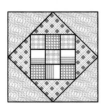

Block 2
Make 4.

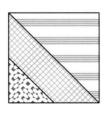

Block 3
Make 4.

Christa by Catherine Hesselin, 1992, Santpoort, The Netherlands, 37½" x 37½".
Dedicated to the memory of
Christa Mekenkamp, Irma's best friend.

Catherine used Dutch farmers' hankies to
piece the back of Christa's quilt.
She appliquéd a Ninepatch block in one of
the hankies for added back interest.

From the ticking, cut:
   2 squares, each 12⅞" x 12⅞". Cut once diagonally
   for Piece F.

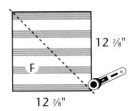

From the medium red fabric, cut:
   16 Template C
   4 Template E

From the dark red fabric, cut:
   4 Template C
   4 Template D

From the black fabric, cut:
   4 Template D

From the reverse side of the black fabric, cut:
   16 Template D

Directions

1. Arrange the 25 light red Template A into 5 rows of 5 squares each. Sew the squares together in horizontal rows, pressing the seams in opposite directions from row to row for easier matching. Sew the rows together to complete the block center.

Press seams in direction of arrows.

Make 1.

2. Add Template C to opposite sides of the block center, then to the remaining 2 sides.

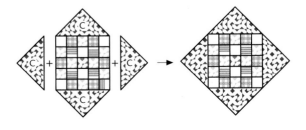

3. Add Template D in the same manner used for adding Template C, to complete Block 1.

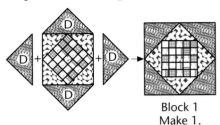

Block 1
Make 1.

4. Arrange 9 light red Template B into 3 rows of 3 blocks each. Sew the squares together in rows, pressing seams in opposite directions from row to row. Sew the rows together to complete the block center. Make 4.

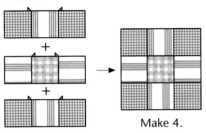

Make 4.

5. Add Templates C and D to each block center to complete 4 of Block 2.

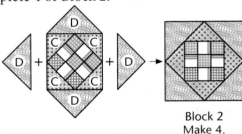

Block 2
Make 4.

6. Assemble 4 Block 3 as shown.

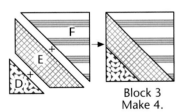

Block 3
Make 4.

7. Referring to the quilt plan on page 25, arrange the finished blocks in 3 rows of 3 blocks each. Stitch the blocks together in rows, pressing the seams in opposite directions from row to row. Sew the rows together to complete the quilt top.

Quilt Finishing

Refer to the general directions for quilt finishing, beginning on page 86.
1. Layer the quilt top with batting and backing; baste.
2. Quilt as desired.
3. Bind edges with strips cut from the red-and-white checked fabric.

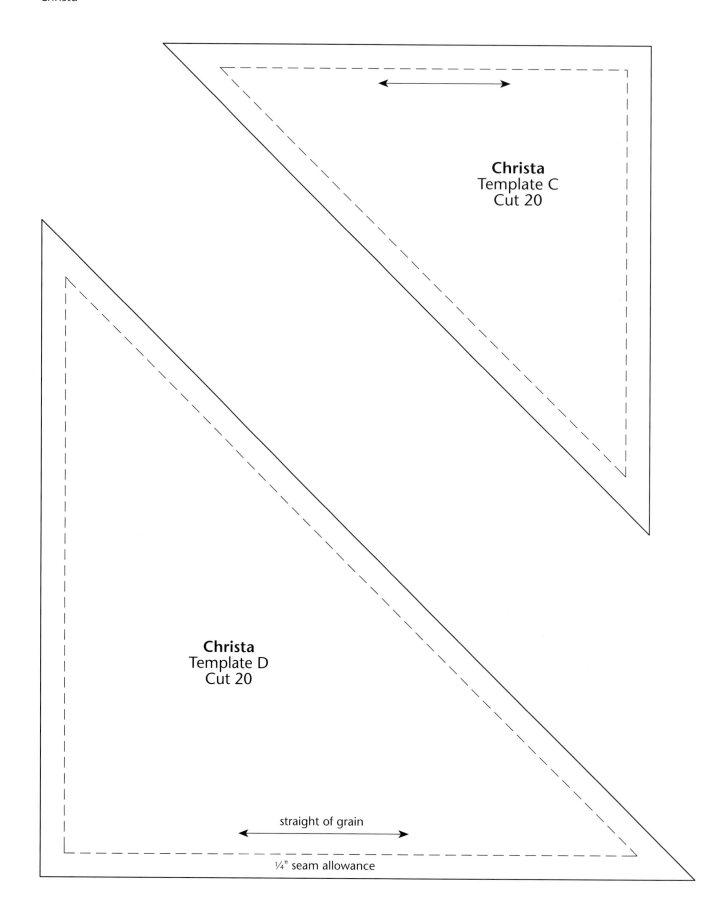

Christa
Template C
Cut 20

Christa
Template D
Cut 20

straight of grain

¼" seam allowance

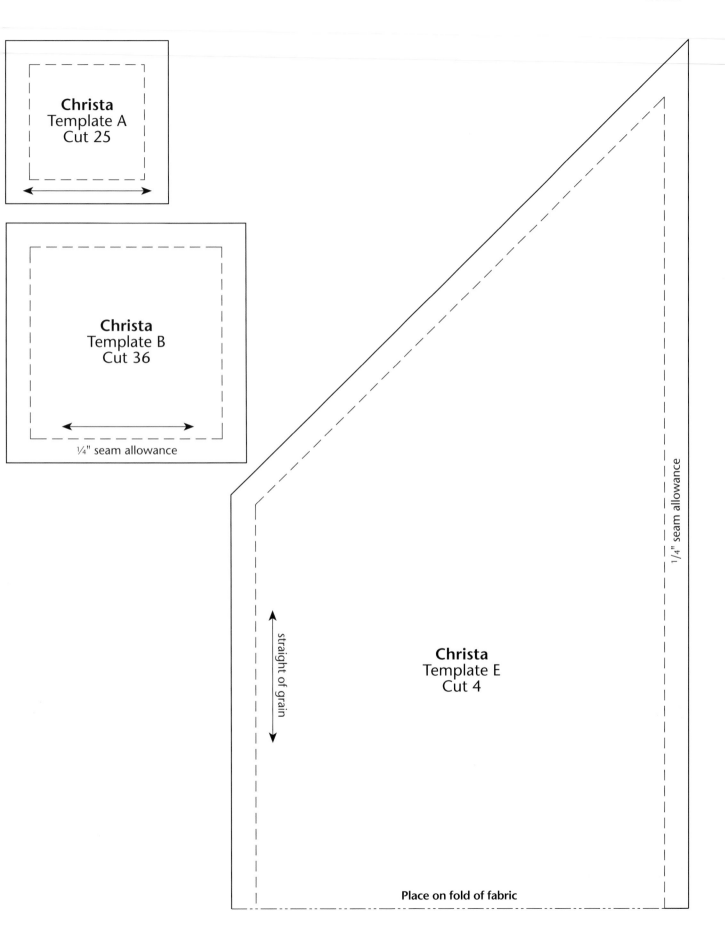

Christa
Template A
Cut 25

Christa
Template B
Cut 36

¼" seam allowance

¼" seam allowance

straight of grain

Christa
Template E
Cut 4

Place on fold of fabric

Dutch Bouquet

BY HELEEN ATEN

FINISHED SIZE: 18" x 18"

Dutch Bouquet by Heleen Aten, 1993, Haarlem, The Netherlands, 18" x 18". Heleen appliquéd bright tulips on a blue background in tribute to the Netherlands' most well-known flower.

𝒴ou can use this pattern to make two very different projects. Make the colorful appliquéd square for a wall hanging or pillow top, or try it in white-on-white with quilting and trapunto. Either way, you can enjoy one of the Netherlands' well-known symbols—the tulip.

The appliqué and quilting patterns given on pages 32 and 33 are each one-quarter of the complete block. Special tulip quilting patterns appear on page 31.

Appliquéd Dutch Bouquet

The appliqué block features blue-green apron fabric from Bunschoten and red sheeting from Spakenburg, two regions of the Netherlands. You may substitute similar fabrics for these.

Materials

1 square of unbleached muslin, 19½" x 19½"
Scraps of blue-green fabric
Scraps of solid dark red, bright red, and
   dark blue fabric
Freezer paper
Hand sewing thread
Appliqué needle
Finishing materials of your choice

Directions

Use the pattern on page 32.

1. Fold the square of muslin in half and then in half again. Press light creases to mark the center and the quarters of the square.

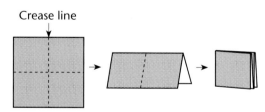

Crease line

2. Using a sharp pencil, trace the pattern on page 32 onto the square. Be sure to line up the dashed lines on the pattern with the creases on the fabric square.

3. Cut and prepare 4 each of the appliqué templates from the appropriate fabrics, referring to the photo above for color placement and referring to directions for freezer-paper appliqué on page 83.

4. Appliqué pieces in numerical order as shown in pattern on page 32.

5. Finish the square as a wall hanging with batting and backing, or use it to make a pillow cover. This large block would also be beautiful as the medallion in the center of a large quilt.

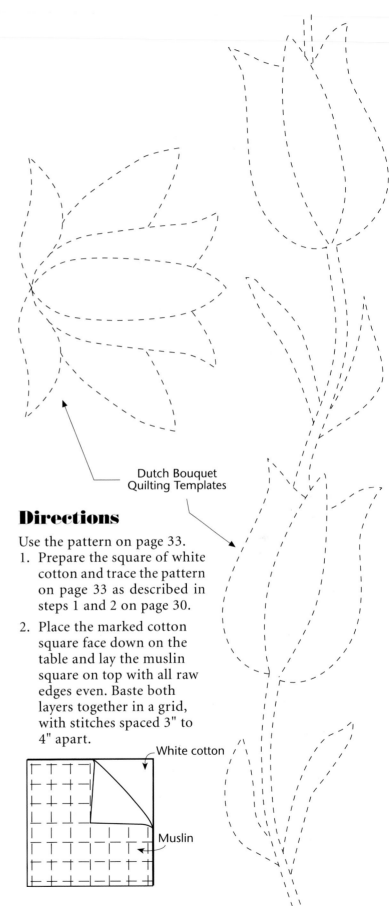

Dutch Bouquet
Quilting Templates

White-on-White Dutch Bouquet by Heleen Aten, 1993, Haarlem, The Netherlands, 18"x 18". Heleen adapted the design for her appliquéd Dutch Bouquet to do white-on-white quilting for a cushion cover or wall hanging.

White-on-White Dutch Bouquet

This lovely block is quilted in a style called trapunto. Small areas of the design are stuffed from the back with yarn or fiberfill to add dimension to the finished piece. You can make this into a wall hanging or pillow cover.

Materials

1 square, 19½" x 19½", of white cotton
1 square, 19½ " x 19½", of loosely woven muslin
Strong white sewing thread
Sharp needle
Fine white cord
Tapestry needle
Polyester fiberfill
Finishing materials of your choice

Directions

Use the pattern on page 33.
1. Prepare the square of white cotton and trace the pattern on page 33 as described in steps 1 and 2 on page 30.

2. Place the marked cotton square face down on the table and lay the muslin square on top with all raw edges even. Baste both layers together in a grid, with stitches spaced 3" to 4" apart.

White cotton

Muslin

31

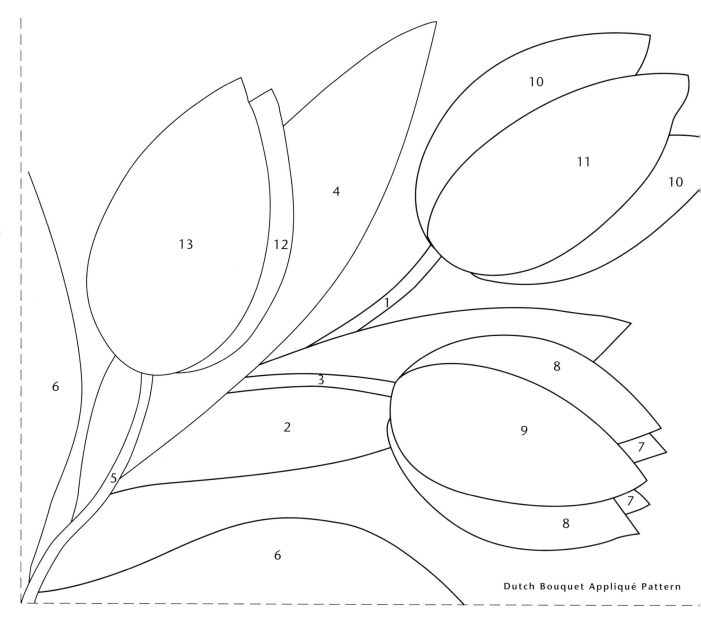

Dutch Bouquet Appliqué Pattern

3. Stitch through both layers of fabric along the marked solid design lines and the dashed lines, as shown, right, using tiny, even stitches. Remove the basting.

4. Working from the muslin side, fill the narrow channels created by the stitching with fine white cord. Thread a blunt-pointed tapestry needle with the cord and insert it through the backing only. After guiding the yarn through the backing, cut the yarn at both ends.

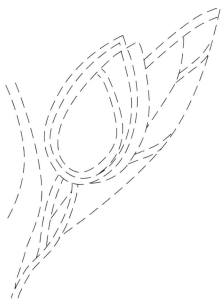

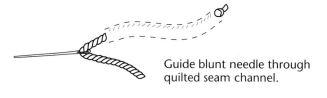

Guide blunt needle through quilted seam channel.

Dutch Bouquet Trapunto Pattern

5. To add dimension to the larger areas of the design, separate the threads of the backing in the area to be stuffed, or make a small slit in the backing only. Insert tiny bits of fiberfill to pad the area to the desired thickness. Be careful not to overstuff.

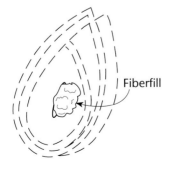

Fiberfill

If you made slits in the backing, loosely whipstitch the edges together to keep the fiberfill in place.

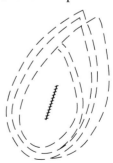

Whipstitch opening closed.

6. Quilt the background in diagonal rows spaced ¼" apart.
7. Finish the square as a wall hanging or pillow cover.

33

Tempo Doeloe

BY BETTEKE BOELE-VOGELESANG

FINISHED SIZE: 42¼" x 43¼"

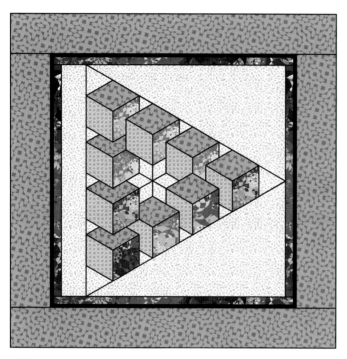

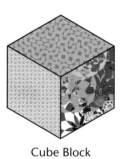

Cube Block

I named this quilt "Tempo Doeloe" for good reason. It is Indonesian for "good old days." I made it for my parents to commemorate their fiftieth wedding anniversary.

One day at a flea market, I bought two old sarongs made of Indonesian batik fabrics. When I showed them to my father, they evoked memories of his childhood in Indonesia as well as the time he lived there with my mother. I decided then and there to use the sarong fabrics in the anniversary quilt. The brown and yellow ochre colors were a perfect match for the color scheme in my parents' home. What's more, one of the batiks was a bird print, very appropriate because the family name—Vogelesang—means birdsong.

I needed more batik fabrics than those in the two sarongs, so I placed an ad in our local newspaper. As a result, a woman donated several sarongs that had belonged to her mother-in-law. She graciously allowed me to use them in my quilt because

it would have been in the style of her mother-in-law to make someone feel happy.

In the back of my mind, I was watching for a pattern that would please my parents. The design inspiration came from a drawing by Oscar Reutersvärd. My father is very much intrigued by these "impossible figures," so I set out to construct a patchwork pattern. I chose a traditional design for the other side of the quilt in my mother's style—warm and cozy. The pattern had to be fairly easy because it was a first-time quilting project for my sister Ingrid and my sister-in-law Hannie. They each made two Ohio stars for Mother's side of the quilt. The center star reads, "50" and includes my parents' names. The names of their children and grandchildren are embroidered in the other stars.

Now that you know the story behind this quilt, I think you will agree that "Tempo Doeloe" was the right choice to commemorate these very happy good (old) days.

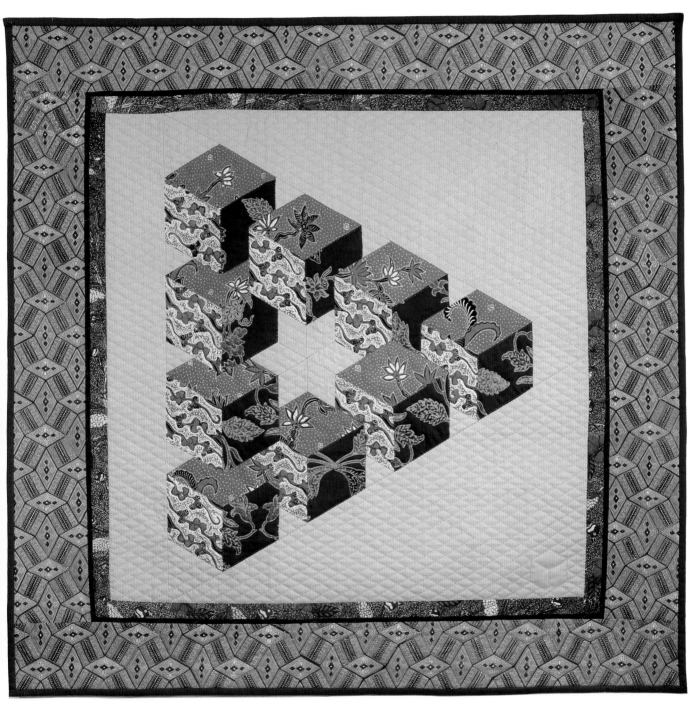

Tempo Doeloe by Betteke Boele-Vogelesang, 1993, Nieuw Vennep, The Netherlands, 41½" x 42½".
Betteke made this anniversary quilt for her parents, using Java print fabrics.

Note: Directions are given only for the front of this quilt. If you wish to make your quilt reversible like mine, make 5 Ohio Star (10") blocks and 4 Hourglass (10") blocks from the desired fabrics. Assemble them, referring to the photo of the quilt back on page 39. Add borders to make the dimensions of the quilt back match the dimensions of the front.

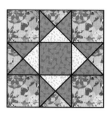
Ohio Star

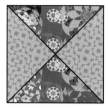
Hourglass

Materials: 44"-WIDE FABRIC

⅓ yd. each of a dark, medium, and light fabric for the cubes
1¼ yds. for background
¼ yd. medium-dark for inner border
⅛ yd. dark for middle border
¾ yd. medium for outer border
1¼ yds. for backing
½ yd. for binding
45" x 45" piece of batting

Cutting

Use the templates on pages 39–40.

From the dark fabric, cut:
5 Template A
2 Template B
1 Template C
1 Template D

From the medium fabric, cut:
5 Template A
2 Template B
1 Template C
1 Template D

From the light fabric, cut:
5 Template A
2 Template B
1 Template C
1 Template D

From the background fabric, cut:
6 Template E
9 Template F
3 Template G
1 strip, 3½" x 30½", for piece H
Set the remaining background fabric aside for the background setting triangles, Piece I (step 3 in "Quilt Top Assembly," on page 38).

From the medium-dark fabric for inner border, cut:
4 strips, each 1½" wide, cutting across the fabric width.

From the dark fabric for the middle border, cut:
4 strips, each ⅞" wide, cutting across the fabric width.

From the medium fabric for the outer border, cut:
4 strips, each 5½" wide, cutting across the fabric width.*
*If your fabric is less than 43" wide, you may need to cut an additional strip.

Directions

While hand piecing is recommended for these complex blocks with many inside corners, you can machine piece if you prefer. Machine stitch in the direction of the arrows for best results and easier piecing.

1. Mark all seam intersections with dots on the wrong side of all cube and background pieces. (See page 80.)

2. Assemble Cubes 1, 2, and 9, following the piecing diagrams for each cube. Stitch in the direction of the arrows to make the piecing easier, ending stitching at the seam intersection of all inside corners, indicated by dots in the illustrations.

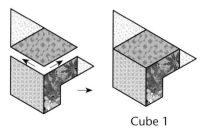
Cube 1

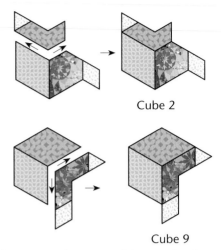

Cube 2

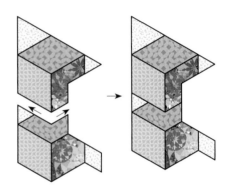

Cube 9

3. Sew Cube 1 to Cube 2, stitching in the direction of the arrows and beginning the stitching at the dot marking the seam intersection.

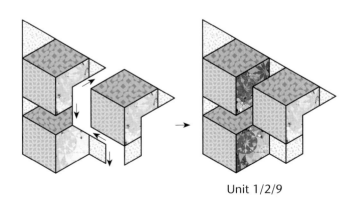

4. Add Cube 9 to the unit.

Unit 1/2/9

5. Assemble Cubes 3, 4, and 5, following the piecing diagrams for each cube.

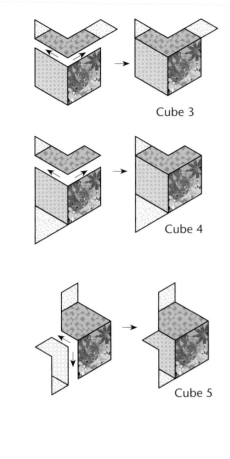

Cube 3

Cube 4

Cube 5

6. Sew Cube 3 to Cube 5.

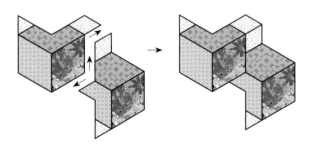

7. Add Cube 4 to the unit.

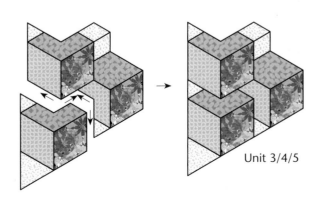

Unit 3/4/5

8. Assemble Cubes 6, 7, and 8, following the piecing diagrams for each cube.

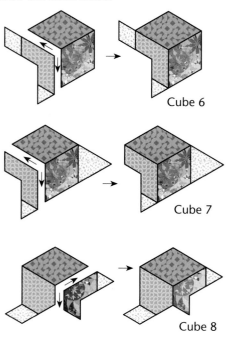

Cube 6

Cube 7

Cube 8

9. Sew Cube 6 to Cube 8.

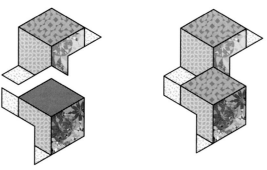

10. Add Cube 7 to the unit.

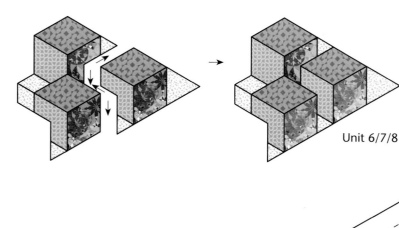

Unit 6/7/8

Quilt Top Assembly

1. Join Unit 1/2/9 to Unit 3/4/5.
2. Add Unit 6/7/8.

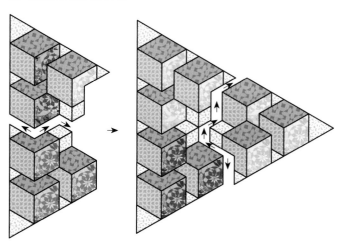

3. Draft a full-size pattern for Piece I, referring to the illustration below for dimensions only. From the remaining background fabric, cut 2 triangles. Be sure to cut 1 and 1 reversed.

4. Sew the triangles to the completed cube unit. Add background strip H to the left-hand side.

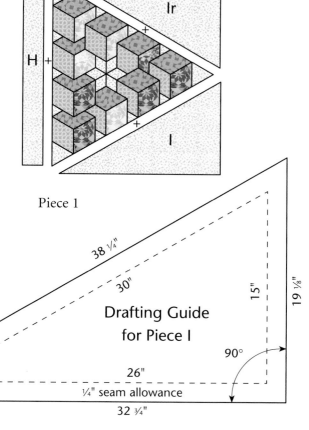

Piece 1

Drafting Guide for Piece I

38°¼"
30"
26"
15"
19 ⅛"
90°
¼" seam allowance
32 ¾"

38

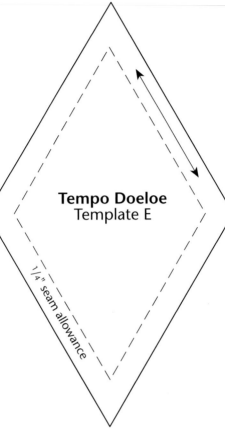

Tempo Doeloe
Template E

1/4" seam allowance

On the back of Tempo Doeloe, Ohio Star and Hourglass blocks contain the names of family members. The blocks were made by Betteke's sister and sister-in-law, who are not quilters.

5. Add the inner side border strips to the quilt top, then the inner top and bottom border strips, following the directions for "Borders with Straight-Cut Corners" on page 85. Repeat with the middle and outer border strips.

Quilt Finishing

Refer to the general directions for quilt finishing, beginning on page 86.

1. Layer the quilt top with batting and backing; baste.
2. Quilt as desired.
3. Bind the edges.

Tempo Doeloe
Template B

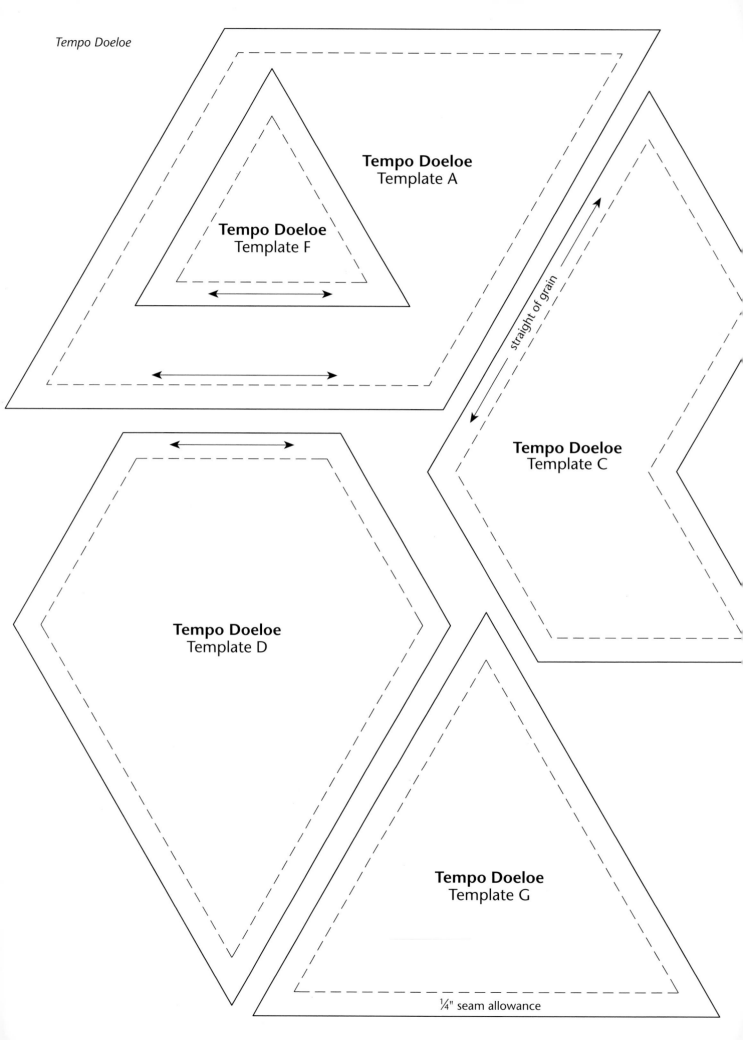

Tempo Doeloe

Tempo Doeloe
Template A

Tempo Doeloe
Template F

straight of grain

Tempo Doeloe
Template C

Tempo Doeloe
Template D

Tempo Doeloe
Template G

¼" seam allowance

Reflexion

BY NEL MEIJER

FINISHED SIZE: 93" x 93"

*I*rma asked me to make a quilt from checked and striped fabrics. "Reflexion," a bargello-style quilt, is the result. This stunning quilt that looks like a butterfly is definitely not for beginners.

Reflexion by Nel Meijer, 1993, Badhoevedorp, The Netherlands, 93" x 93". This dramatic quilt was strip-pieced, bargello style, and made in sections. When joined, they create the impression of a grand butterfly.

Materials: 44"-WIDE FABRIC

- 1½ yds. Color A1
- 2 yds. Color A2*
- 1¼ yds. Color B
- 1⅜ yds. Color C1
- 1 yd. Color C2
- 2½ yds. Color D
- 1¾ yds. Color E
- 1¼ yds. Color F

Also: ⅜ yd. for binding
6 yds. for backing
96" x 96" piece of batting

*In the quilt shown, Colors A1 and A2 were cut from the same striped fabric, with the strips for A1 cut on the lengthwise grain and the strips for A2 cut on the crosswise grain. The same is true for colors C1 and C2. If you wish to do this in your quilt too, combine yardages for A1 and A2 and for C1 and C2. Otherwise, choose 2 different fabrics in the same color range for each color pair.

This quilt is made of 4 identical quarters.

Each quarter has 2 equal halves divided by a center row. You will make this quilt in 8 sections of 36 rows each and then join them in pairs with a center strip.

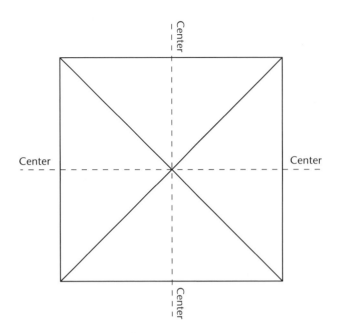

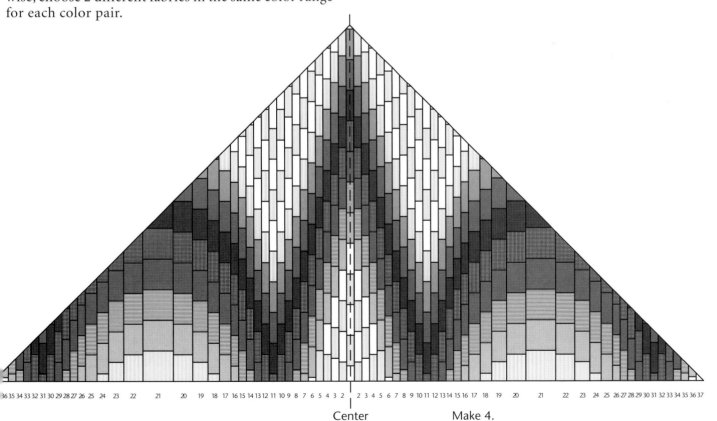

Center   Make 4.

43

Directions

Strip Unit Cutting and Assembly

1. For the center rows of each section, cut the following 4½" x 6" strips from the fabrics indicated and label strips appropriately.

Fabric	No. of Strips
A1	4
A2	2
B	1
C1	1
C2	1
D	2
E	1
F	1

2. Sew the strips together as shown along the longest edges. Cut 4 strips, each 1½" wide, from the strip-pieced unit. Label each strip as a center strip and set aside.

3. For Row 2, cut the following 4½" x 6" strips from the fabrics indicated.

Fabric	No. of Strips
A1	4
A2	6
B	2
C1	2
C2	2
D	4
E	2
F	2

4. Sew the strips together in 2 identical strip units as shown. Cut 4 strips, each 1½" wide, from each unit for a total of 8. Label as Row 2 and set aside.

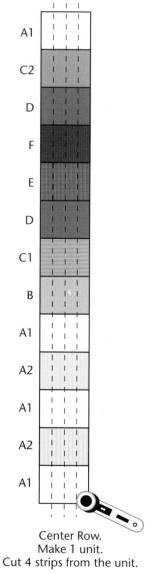

Center Row.
Make 1 unit.
Cut 4 strips from the unit.

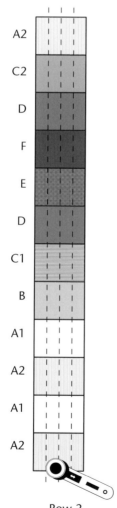

Row 2.
Make 2 units.
Cut 4 strips from each unit.

5. Continue making strip units in the same fashion for Rows 3–16, and Rows 26–36, referring to the illustration below to determine the color progression and the number of strips to cut for the strip unit. Cut all strips for these rows 4½" x 6" and make 2 strip units of each.

   Cut 4 strips, each 1½" wide, from each strip-pieced unit for a total of 8 strips, one for each of the 8 sections of the quilt. Label each strip with the appropriate row number.

   Note: Use full strip widths for the colors at the top and bottom of each row. When you arrange the strips in their proper orientation, you will cut off excess strip length at the top or bottom, or both. (See illustration with steps 2 and 3 on page 46.)

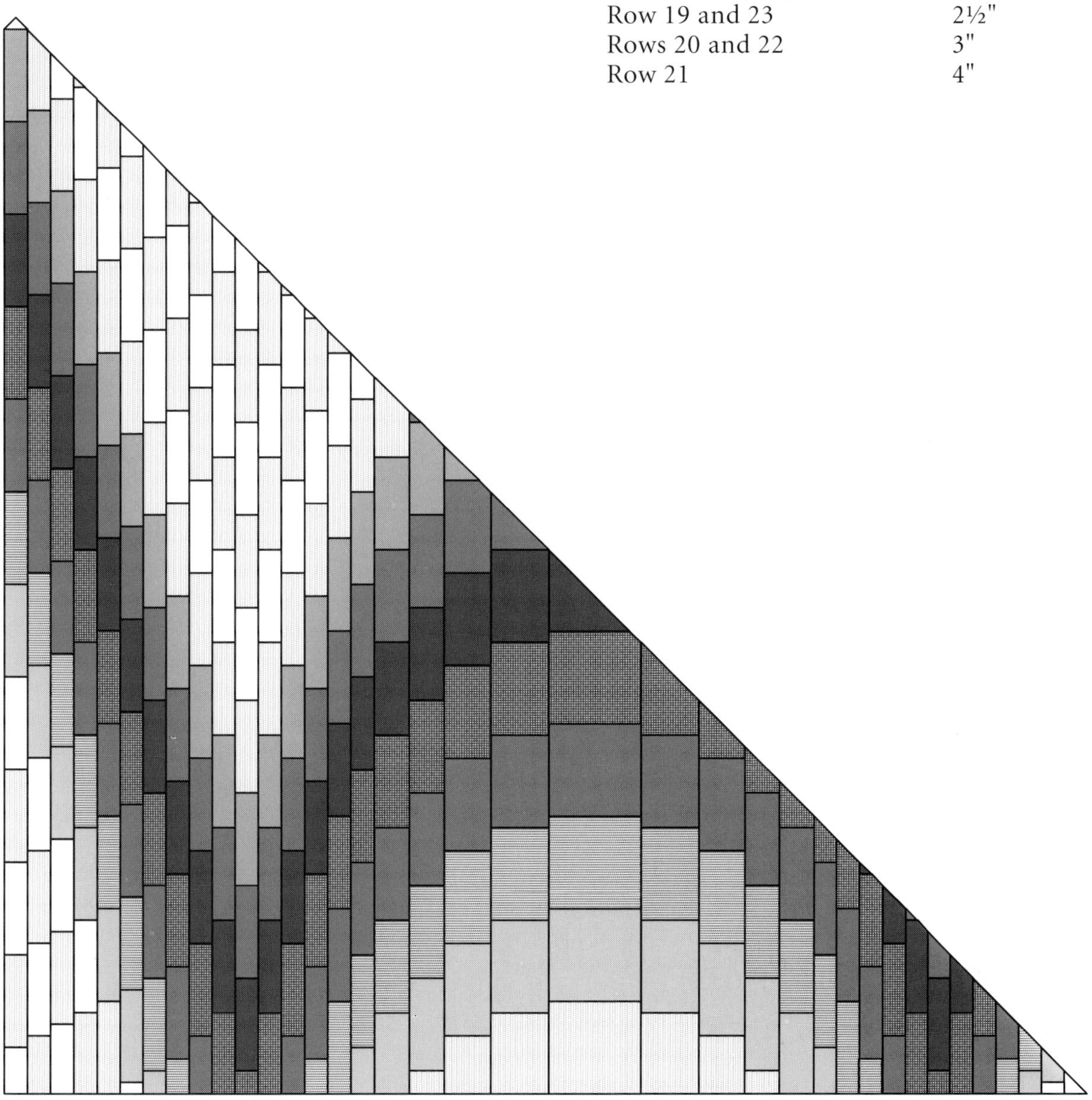

6. Make 2 strip units for each of Rows 17–25. Cut strips the dimension given in the chart below. Refer to the illustration for color placement and the number of each required for each row.

Row	Strip Dimensions
Rows 17, 18, 24, 25, and 37	4½" x 8"
Rows 19 and 23	4½" x 10"
Rows 20 and 22	4½" x 12"
Row 21	4½" x 16"

   Cut each strip unit into 4 strips, cutting them the width indicated in the chart below, for a total of 8 strips of each. Label each strip with the appropriate row number.

Row	Strip Width
Rows 17, 18, 24, 25, and 37	2"
Row 19 and 23	2½"
Rows 20 and 22	3"
Row 21	4"

1 2 3 4 5 6 7 8 9 10 11 12 13 14 15 16 17 18 19 20 21 22 23 24 25 26 27 28 29 30 31 32 33 34 35 36 37

Quilt Top Assembly

1. Referring to the quilt plan, arrange the strips for one-quarter of the quilt (the large triangle on page 43), beginning at the center and working out to the edges. Offset the rows to create the undulating motion. Make sure that the strip positions on each side of the center strip are correctly placed to make a mirror image.

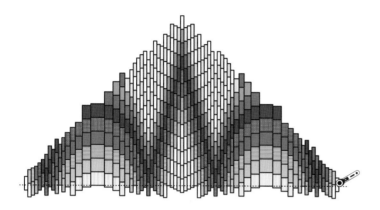

2. Carefully pin and sew the strips together, working from the center out and adding the strips to opposite sides in alternating fashion. Sew and press carefully. Trim away excess length along the bottom edge, making sure that the cut is perpendicular to the vertical-strip seam lines.

3. Make a cut on each side of the piece at a 45° angle, as shown below, making sure that the peak of the triangle will be in the center of the center strip. This must be accurate, so measure and cut with care.

4. Using the first quarter as a pattern, make 3 more identical quarters.

5. Pin the triangles together in pairs, carefully matching the seams. Stitch, being careful not to stretch the bias edges.

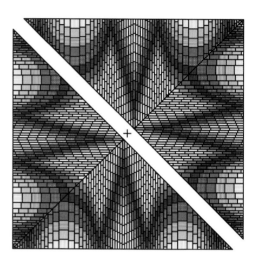

Quilt Finishing

Refer to the general directions for quilt finishing, beginning on page 86.

1. Layer the quilt top with batting and backing; baste.
2. Quilt as desired. (To soften all the straight lines in this quilt, I used a curved quilting pattern.)
3. Bind the edges.

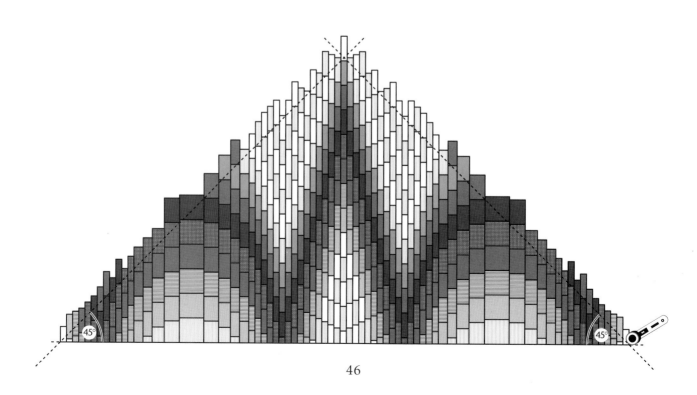

Delft Blue

BY IRMA ESKES

FINISHED SIZE: 24" x 24"
BLOCK SIZE: 12" x 12"

*Delft Blue by Irma Eskes, 1993, Haarlem, The Netherlands, 24" x 24".
Antique Delft blue tiles inspired this tribute to the Dutch tile-making industry.
Thanks to Mr. Mudde for allowing us to photograph this quilt in his antique
shop, next door to Irma's Sampler.*

The first tile works in the Netherlands was established around 1570. Haarlem, where my shop is located, had its own tile works. Influenced by the Crusaders, the images showed Spanish and Italian characteristics. From 1600 on, the designs on the tiles became more naturalistic, with pictures of human beings, animals, and lively scenes depicting Dutch folklore. It was popular to decorate the walls with these beautiful blue-and-white tiles. It not only gave the interior an air of wealth and distinction, it was also durable and hygienic.

The tiles were cut from slabs of clay and after they were dried and baked, they were covered with a layer of white glaze. Then the tile decorator could mark the design. A perforated pattern, called a "sponge," was placed on top of the tile, and charcoal powder was rubbed into the perforations. The tiny black dots were then traced with blue paint to make neat lines. Doesn't this sound very much like one of the methods you can use to transfer a complicated quilting pattern to a quilt top?

We identify Delft tiles as belonging in one of ten different categories. To design my quilt, I chose tiles from four of these categories: Fruit Dish, seventeenth century; Tulip, sixteenth and seventeenth centuries; Flower Vase, seventeenth century; and Animal tile, sixteenth and seventeenth centuries. The designs are decidedly primitive in character, and the corner designs are derived from the French fleur-de-lis. I used seven different authentic blue Dutch fabrics to make this quilt, a tribute to our tile-making heritage. Each of these fabrics is still in use in the Netherlands today. Accents were embroidered with an outline stitch.

Materials: 44"-WIDE FABRIC

1 yd. solid-colored ecru fabric
    for blocks and binding
Assorted blue fabrics in solid
    colors and prints
¾ yd. for backing
27" x 27" piece of batting
Blue embroidery floss

Directions

Use the patterns on the pullout pattern in the back of
this book.

1. Cut 4 squares, each 16" x 16", from the ecru fabric.
   Fold each into quarters and press lightly to mark
   the center of each.

Crease lines

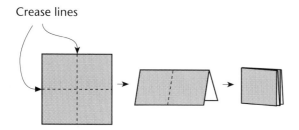

2. Working on a light table or at a window, trace a
   design onto each square, being careful to center the
   design in the square.
3. Using the assorted blue fabrics, prepare the
   appliqué shapes for "Freezer-Paper Appliqué" as
   shown on page 83.
4. Appliqué the shapes in position on each square.
5. Add embroidered accents, using 3 strands of blue
   embroidery floss and the outline stitch.

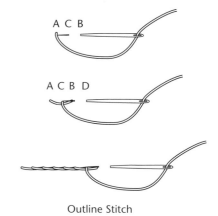

Outline Stitch

6. Arrange the squares in 2 rows of 2 blocks each, following the quilt plan on this page or using an arrangement of your choice. Sew the blocks together
   in 2 horizontal rows. Sew the rows together to complete the quilt top.

Quilt Finishing

Refer to the general directions for quilt finishing, beginning on page 86.

1. Layer the quilt top with batting and backing; baste.
2. Quilt the background as desired.
3. Finish the edges with binding cut from the remaining ecru fabric.

48

Cow Quilt

BY YOLA VAN OJEN

FINISHED SIZE: 23¼" x 32¼"
BLOCK SIZE: 3¾" x 6¾"

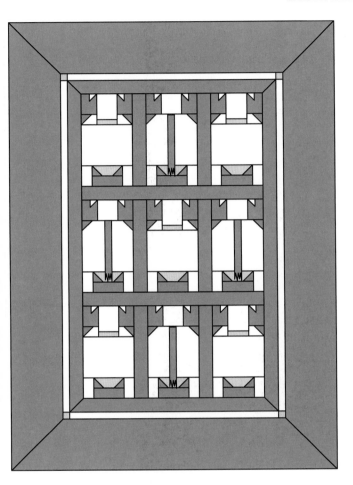

Three years ago, our daughter had the wonderful opportunity to spend a year as an exchange student at a high school in California. All exchange students were given nicknames, and so she became "Dutch Cow." Whenever she writes to her American friends, she always tries to find cow postcards. When Irma asked me to design a Dutch quilt for her book, I knew it had to be one in which cows would play the leading role. My quilt was machine pieced and hand quilted. There are a total of nine blocks—five cows looking you in the face and four swishing their tails at you. Have fun making this whimsical quilt.

Materials: 44"-WIDE FABRIC

1⅛ yds. green for grass, sashing, inner border, outer border, and binding
½ yd. "cow" print
Scraps of pink and black solids
1 yd. for backing
27" x 36" piece of batting

Cutting

Use the templates on pages 53–54.

From the green, cut:
    18 Template A
    36 Template B
    9 Template C
    6 strips, each 1½" x 7¼", for vertical sashing
    2 strips, each 1½" x 13¼", for horizontal sashing
    2 strips, each 1½" x 26¼", for inner side borders*
    2 strips, each 1½" x 17¼", for inner top and
        bottom borders*
    2 strips, each 3¾" x 34", for outer side borders*
    2 strips, each 3¾" x 25", for outer top and
        bottom borders*

*Strips for mitered borders include extra length for mitering. (See pages 84–85.)

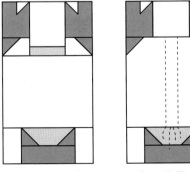

Cow I (Front)   Cow II (Back)

*Cow Quilt by Yola van Ojen, 1993, Haarlem, The Netherlands,
23¼" x 32¼". Yola designed this quilt for her daughter, who received the
nickname "Dutch Cow" during her studies in California.*

From the "cow" print, cut:
  5 Template F
  5 Template G and 5 G reversed
  5 Template H
  18 Template J
  4 Template K
  4 Template L
  18 Template M
  2 strips, each ¾" x 24¾", for middle side borders
  2 strips, each ¾" x 15¾", for middle top and
      bottom borders

From the pink, cut:
  5 Template D
  9 Template E
  4 squares, each ¾" x ¾"

From the black, cut:
  4 strips, each 1" x 5½", for the tails (Piece I)

Directions

1. Using Piece M, make 18 ears. Fold each triangle in half with right sides together and stitch along the bias edge. Turn right side out and press. Set aside. You will add ears to each pieced block later.

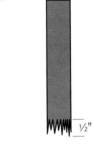

Make 18.

2. Unravel ½" of one end of each of the 4 black tail strips (Piece I).

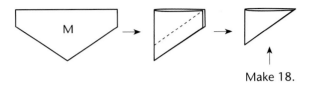

3. Fold each tail strip in half lengthwise with wrong sides together; press. Open the strip and turn the raw edges in to meet in the center of the strip. Whipstitch folded edges together. Set aside.

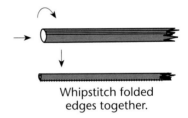

Whipstitch folded edges together.

4. Make 5 Cow I, following piecing diagram below.

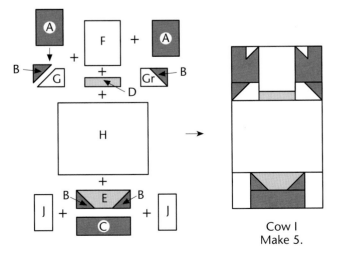

Cow I
Make 5.

5. Position ears on each Cow block and baste in place.

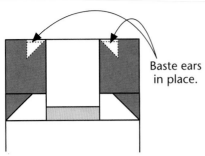

Baste ears in place.

6. Make 4 Cow II, following the piecing diagram below. Catch the tail's raw edge in the seam between the head and the body.

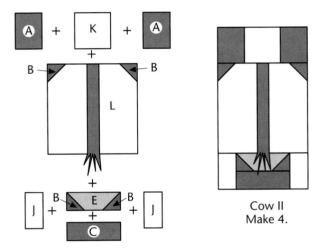

Cow II
Make 4.

Quilt Top Assembly

1. Lay out the blocks and sashing strips as shown.
2. Sew the blocks and vertical sashing strips together in horizontal rows.
3. Join the rows with the horizontal sashing strips.

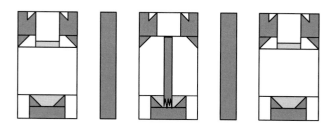

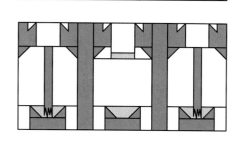

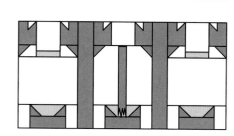

Borders

1. Sew the green inner borders to the quilt top, following the directions on pages 84–85 for borders with mitered corners. Press seams toward the border.
2. Sew the ¾"-wide cow print side border strips to the quilt top. Press seams toward the border.
3. Sew a pink square to each end of the top and bottom cow print border strips. Sew borders to the quilt top.

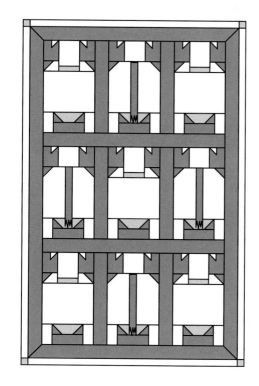

4. Sew the green outer border strips to the quilt, mitering the corners as shown on pages 84–85.

Quilt Finishing

Refer to the general directions for quilt finishing, beginning on page 86.

1. Layer the quilt top with batting and backing; baste.
2. Quilt in-the-ditch around the cows. Quilt tulips in the outer borders, using the tulip pattern below.

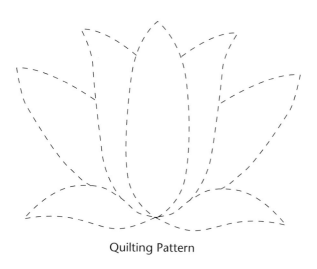

Quilting Pattern

3. Finish the edges with binding cut from the remaining green fabric.

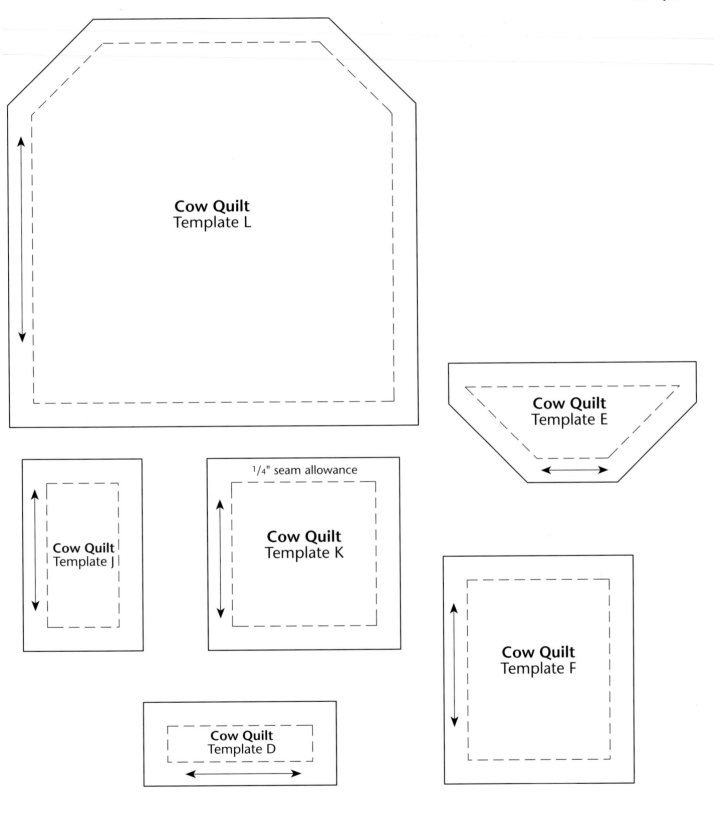

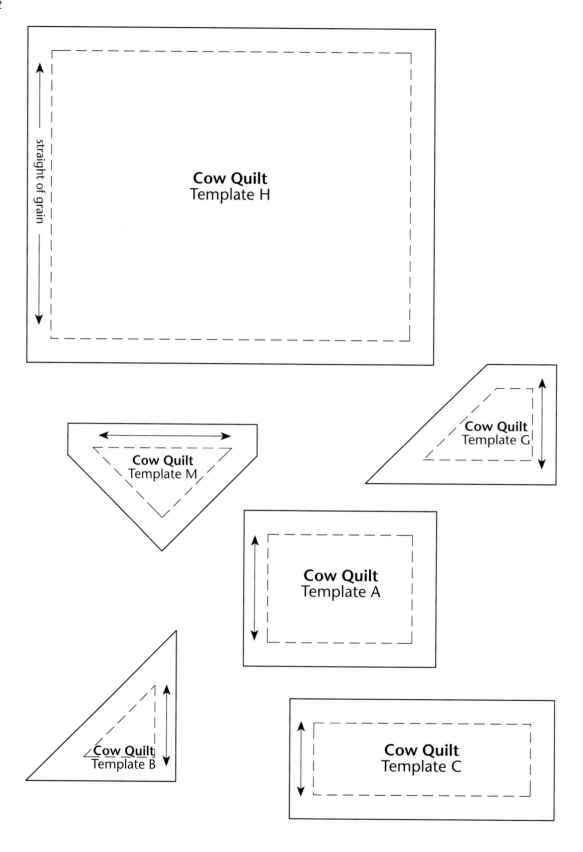

straight of grain

Cow Quilt
Template H

Cow Quilt
Template M

Cow Quilt
Template G

Cow Quilt
Template A

Cow Quilt
Template B

Cow Quilt
Template C

Reversible Quilt

BY YOLA VAN OJEN

FINISHED SIZE: 64" x 79"

A Cow block takes center stage on the reverse side of Yola's colorful quilt.

Reversible Quilt by Yola van Ojen, 1993, Haarlem, The Netherlands, 64" x 79". Yola used typical Dutch cottons in a red-white-and-blue color scheme to create this warm and cozy quilt. With her reversible technique, you can have two quilts in the time it would take to make one!

55

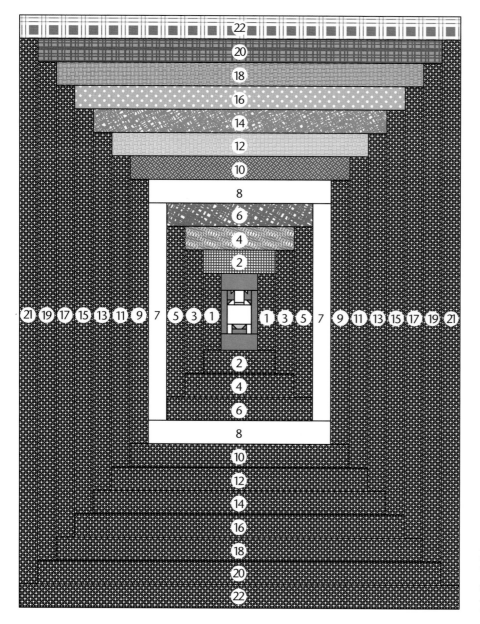

Materials:
44"-WIDE FABRIC

Approximately 6 yds. assorted
   prints for Side A
Approximately 6 yds. assorted
   prints for Side B
1 pieced cow block
   (See pages 49–51.)
1 yd. fabric for binding
4 yds. batting

Note: It is easy to adjust the size of this quilt by using fewer strips or adding more strips as you work your way out from the center block.

*M*aking a reversible quilt has many advantages. It is quick and easy to make two quilts at once since the front and back of the quilt are attached to the batting in one step. When you have completed the top, the quilting is also completed. Of course, you will have two different quilts in one only if you use different fabrics for the front and back.

For Side A, I chose a variety of checks and flower prints, typical Dutch fabrics, all in blue. On Side B, the center is a patchwork cow, made using the pattern on page 49. The strips were cut from blue cow print fabric and from a selection of Dutch farmers' hankies, checks, and flowered sheeting. I cut the binding from the hankies as well. Choose a variety of fabrics in your favorite colors to make your own quilt very special. Make the center a real eye-catcher, using a different patchwork block if you prefer.

Cutting

The strips are numbered for each side of the quilt in the same way. Following the chart below, cut 2 of each strip size for Side A and 2 for Side B. In addition, cut 2 strips of each size from the batting.

It is a good idea to cut all the strips for Side A and label them with their number. Set aside and repeat for the Side B strips. Another option is to cut each set of strips as you need them, rather than cutting them all at once.

Strip	Size	Strip	Size
1	3¼" x 12"	12	4" x 38"
2	4" x 11½"	13	3¼" x 52"
3	3¼" x 18½"	14	4" x 43¼"
4	4" x 16¾"	15	3¼" x 59"
5	3¼" x 25¼"	16	4" x 48½"
6	4" x 22"	17	3¼" x 65½"
7	3¼" x 32"	18	4" x 54"
8	4" x 27½"	19	3¼" x 72"
9	3¼" x 38½"	20	4" x 59"
10	4" x 33"	21	3¼" x 79"
11	3¼" x 45"	22	4" x 64¼"

Directions

1. Make a patchwork cow block for the center of Side B, using the templates on pages 53–54. To extend the finished block to the required size, cut 2 strips, each 1⅜" x 7¼", for the sides, and 2 strips, each 2⅞" x 6", for the top and bottom. Sew the strips to the sides and then to the top and bottom.

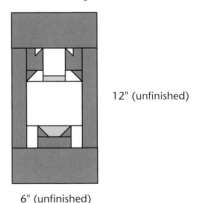

12" (unfinished)

6" (unfinished)

Note: You may substitute another block or a colorful panel of your choice, but its outer dimensions must measure 6" x 12" (5½" x 11½" finished size).

2. For the center of Side A, cut a 6" x 12" piece of fabric. Cut a piece of batting the same size.

3. Place the center piece for Side B face down on the table. Add the batting center and then the center piece for Side A, right side up. Pin in place and machine zigzag all around the edges.

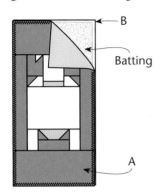

B

Batting

A

4. Layer Strip #1 for Side A and Side B with the center panel and a matching strip of batting as shown. Pin and stitch ¼" from the raw edges. Repeat with the remaining Strip #1 pieces.

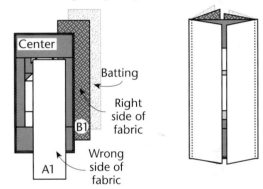

Center

Batting

Right side of fabric

B1

Wrong side of fabric

A1

Note: To avoid confusion, always work with the pieces for Side B against the table.

5. Open out the strips and batting. Pin the raw edges together and join them with a zigzag stitch. Zigzag the long edges first, then the short ones, stitching from the outer corner in.

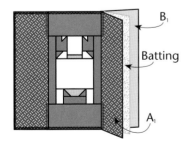

B₁

Batting

A₁

6. Continue adding strips in numerical order as shown on the quilt plan.

7. Bind the edges. See pages 86–88.

Feathers

BY MARIET STOUTENBEEK

FINISHED SIZE: 58" x 81½"

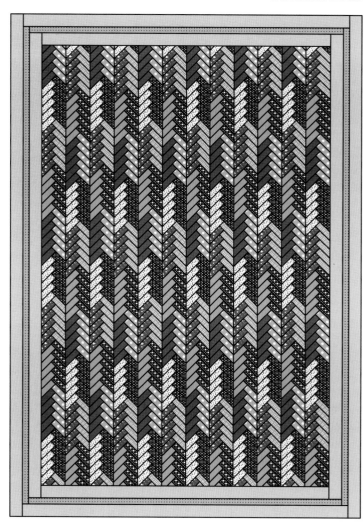

*O*ur quilt group decided to make this quilt using the traditional brick design. It didn't look too complicated and it could be executed in many different ways, depending on the colors you chose and how you arranged them. This quilt is beautiful done in scraps, too, rather than in a coordinated color scheme. Try it in Christmas colors for a special holiday quilt.

I used scraps from another project and added a variety of typical red-and-white and blue-and-white Dutch fabrics. When you sew the "bricks" together for this quilt, red fabrics are always combined with red-and-white fabrics and blue with blue-and-white fabrics. Although it looks complicated, it is very easy to stitch the rows of bricks together in strips without stitching any inside corners!

Materials: 44"-WIDE FABRIC

Assorted scraps in red, red-and-white, blue, and blue-and-white prints
2¾ yds. red solid for inner and outer borders and binding
4¾ yds. blue solid for borders and backing

Cutting

Use the template on page 61, or if you prefer rotary cutting, cut fabric into 1½"-wide strips. Then cut the strips into 3½"-long bricks.

For each of the 6 odd rows, cut:
    25 red bricks
    25 red/white bricks
    25 blue/white bricks
    25 blue bricks

For each of the 6 even rows, cut:
    25 blue
    25 blue/white bricks
    25 red/white bricks
    25 red
Note: Wait to cut border strips until you have completed the piecing.

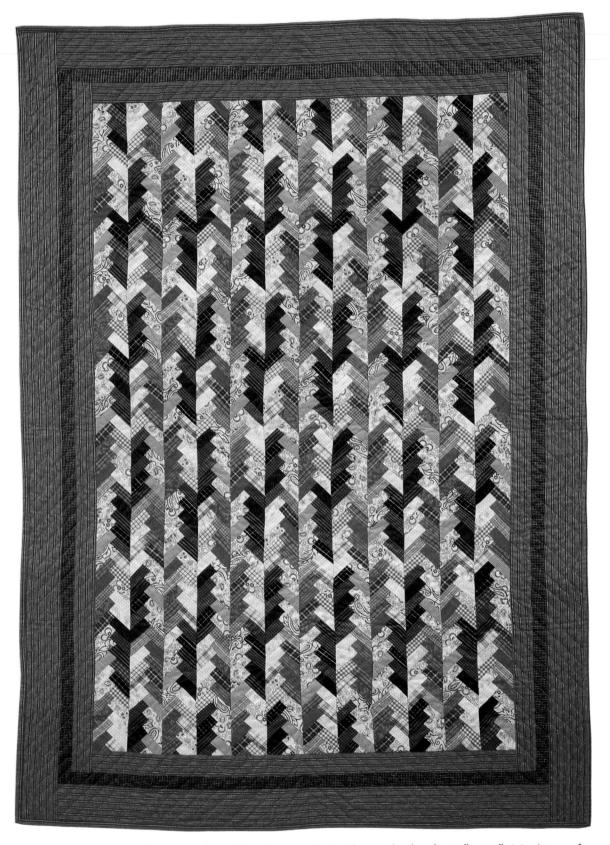

Feathers by Mariet Stoutenbeek, 1993, Bloemendaal, The Netherlands, 56" x 82". Mariet used Dutch Village fabrics to create this traditional brick-style quilt.

Directions

Odd Rows 1, 3, 5, 7, 9, and 11

1. Place a blue-and-white brick right side up on the table and place a blue brick on top, right sides together and raw edges matching. Stitch. Press the seam toward the blue brick.

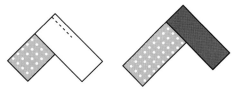

2. Place the next blue-and-white brick on top of the completed unit and stitch as shown. Press the seam toward the blue-and-white brick.

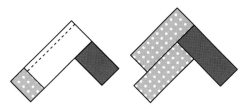

3. Place the next blue brick on top of the completed unit and stitch as shown. Press the seam toward the blue brick.

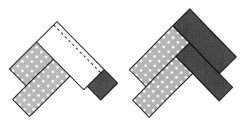

4. Continue adding blue-and-white and blue bricks in the same manner until you have a total of 5 bricks of each color in the unit.

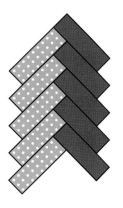

5. Repeat steps 1–4 with red and red-and-white bricks.

6. Continue in this manner, alternating sets of bricks until the strip contains 50 two-brick units.
7. Make 5 more strips in this manner.

Even Rows 2, 4, 6, 8, 10, and 12

1. Place a red-and-white brick right side up on the table and place a red brick on top, right sides together and raw edges matching. Stitch. Press the seam toward the red brick.

2. Place the next red-and-white brick on top of the completed unit and stitch as shown. Press the seam toward the red-and-white brick.

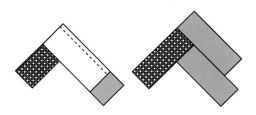

3. Place the next red brick on top of the completed unit and stitch as shown.

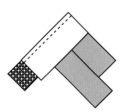

4. Continue adding red-and-white and red bricks in the same manner until you have a total of 5 bricks of each color in the unit.
5. Add 5 sets of blue and blue-and-white bricks in the same manner.

6. Continue in this manner, with alternating sets of bricks until the strip contains 50 two-brick units.
7. Make 5 more rows in this manner.

Quilt Top Assembly

1. On each strip, place the 45° line of a rotary ruler on a seam line of one of the strip units as shown, with the edge of the ruler at the corner where two bricks meet. Trim excess away with the rotary cutter. Repeat on the other edge of the strip.
   Note: Only a partial strip is shown in the illustration at right.

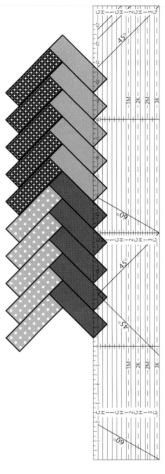

2. Sew the vertical rows together, alternating odd and even rows. Pin carefully so seams match. Stitch.
3. Measure the quilt for straight-cut borders as shown on page 85, measuring for the top and bottom borders first. Cutting along the lengthwise grain of the fabric, cut 2"-wide red border strips to fit and stitch to the top and bottom edges of the quilt. Measure for and add the side borders in the same manner.
4. Measure for and add the blue middle border and the red outer border strips in the same manner, attaching the top and bottom borders first and then the side borders in each case.

Quilt Finishing

Refer to the general directions for quilt finishing, beginning on page 86.
1. Layer the quilt top with batting and backing; baste.
2. Quilt as desired.
3. Bind the edges with strips cut from the remaining red solid fabric.

Red, White, and Blue

BY WIL VUIJK

FINISHED SIZE: 36¼" x 37¼"

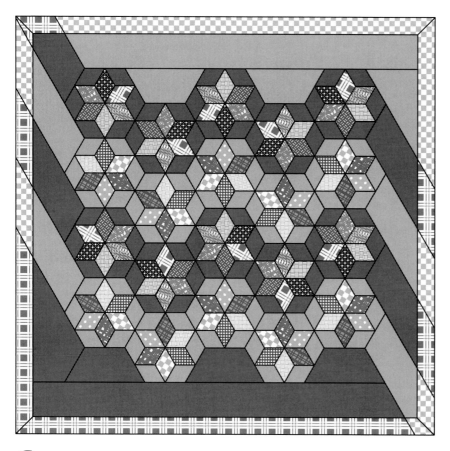

Materials: 44"-WIDE FABRIC

1 yd. blue solid (Block 1)

2½" x 26" strip of each of 3 different dark blue prints (Block 1)

2½" x 26" strip of each of 3 different light blue prints (Block 1)

1 yd. red solid (Block 2)

2½" x 26" strip of 3 different dark red prints (Block 2)

2½" x 26" strip of 3 different light red prints (Block 2)

10" x 36" strip of blue checked fabric for border

10" x 36" strip of red checked fabric for border

1¼ yds. blue checked fabric for backing

½ yd. blue checked fabric for binding

40" x 40" piece of batting

I actually made this quilt for the annual quilt show of the Dutch Quiltersgilde. However, it was never exhibited, because by the time I finally finished my quilt, it was far beyond the registration closing date.

I decided to use only Dutch fabrics and started to make stars from Dutch prints. Next, I added solid blue and solid red diamonds to make hexagons. With a bit of juggling, this setting emerged.

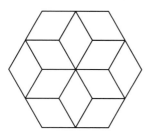

Hexagon Block

Cutting

Use the templates on the pullout pattern sheet in the back of this book.

Block 1

From the blue solid, cut 60 Template A.

From each of the 3 different dark blue prints, cut 10 Template A, for a total of 30 pieces.

From each of the 3 different light blue prints, cut 10 Template A, for a total of 30 pieces.

Block 2

From the red solid, cut 60 Template A.

From each of the 3 different dark red prints, cut 10 Template A, for a total of 30 pieces.

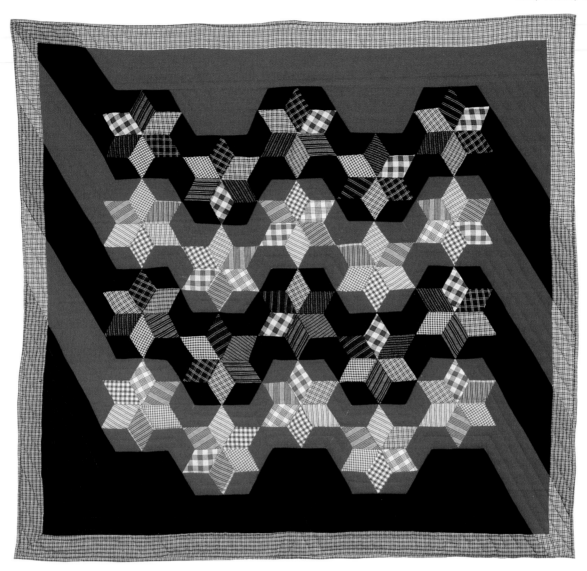

Red, White, and Blue by Wil Vuyk, 1993, Alphen aan de Rijn, The Netherlands, 36¾" x 37¾". Wil made this wonderful quilt, using Dutch fabrics and a traditional hexagon star pattern. Notice the transparency effects she achieved by stretching color into the borders.

From each of the 3 different light red prints,
cut 10 Template A, for a total of 30 pieces.

Fill-in Pieces

From the blue solid, cut:
   3 Template B
   1 Template C
   3 Template D
   1 Template E
   1 Template H

From the red solid, cut:
   2 Template B
   3 Template D
   1 Template F
   1 Template G
   1 Template I

Border

From the blue checked fabric for the border, cut:
   1 Template J for the left-hand border
   1 Template K for the left-hand border and
      2 for the right-hand border
   1 Template L for the left-hand border
   1 Template M for the upper border
   1 Template O for the bottom border

From the red checked fabric for the border, cut:
   1 Template K for the right-hand border and
      2 for the left-hand border
   1 Template Q for the right-hand border
   1 Template R for the right-hand border
   1 Template P for the bottom border
   1 Template N for the top border

Directions

Blocks

1. Using a sharp pencil, mark dots at all seam intersections on diamonds cut from Template A. (See page 80.)

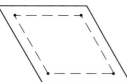

2. Arrange the pieces for 10 blue blocks (Block 1) and 10 red blocks (Block 2), following the diagram and alternating the light and dark pieces. Sew each block together, following steps 3–6.

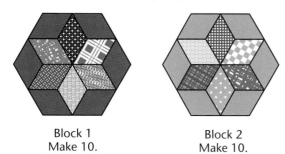

Block 1
Make 10.

Block 2
Make 10.

3. Sew 2 Template A together, beginning and ending the stitching at the marked seam intersections.

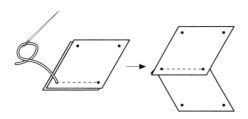

4. Add the third Template A to make a half star.

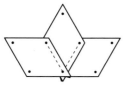

Half Star

5. Repeat steps 3 and 4 to make the remaining half star.

6. Sew the star halves together, being careful not to sew past the marked seam intersections so the seam allowances remain free for easier pressing. Press all seams in one direction.

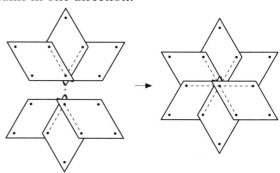

7. Set in the corner pieces (blue solid or red solid Template A), carefully matching the seam-allowance dots and pivoting at the set-in corners. Press the seams toward the corner pieces.

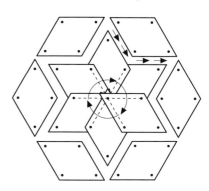

Quilt Top Assembly

1. Arrange the blocks and the fill-in pieces cut from Template B, following the quilt plan and referring to the photo on page 63 for color placement.
2. Sew the blocks and pieces together in vertical rows, beginning and ending the stitching at the seam intersections.

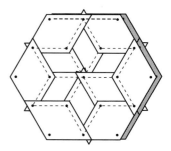

3. Sew the rows together, pivoting at inside corners.

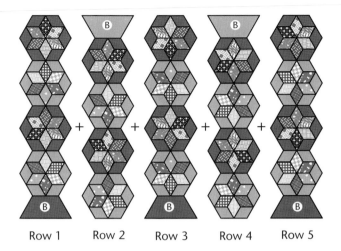

Row 1   Row 2   Row 3   Row 4   Row 5

4. Add the remaining pieces (Templates C, D, E, F, and G) to the left- and right-hand sides of the quilt. Begin at the bottom, working from the bottom up on the right-hand side and from the top down on the left-hand side. As you add each piece, pivot the stitching at the inside corners.

Add pieces, working from top to bottom.

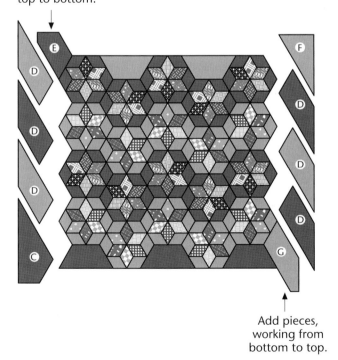

Add pieces, working from bottom to top.

5. Add Template I to the top edge of the quilt and Template H to the bottom edge of the quilt.

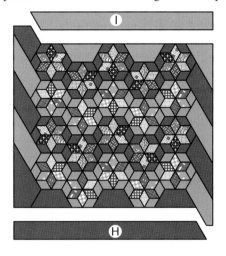

6. Assemble the border strips as shown in the diagrams below.

Note: Templates J and L–R are all extra long to allow for mitering corners. When joining top strip M/N to quilt top, pin securely so seam intersections match at E/I. Then pin remaining border strip in place. Excess border will extend at each end. Stitch. When joining bottom border O/P to quilt top, pin securely to match seams at G/H. Continue as described for strip M/N.

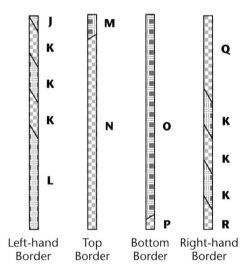

Left-hand   Top   Bottom   Right-hand
Border   Border   Border   Border

7. Sew the border strips to the quilt top, mitering the corners as shown on pages 84–85.

Quilt Finishing

Refer to the general directions for quilt finishing, beginning on page 86.
1. Layer the quilt top with batting and backing; baste.
2. Quilt as desired.
3. Bind the edges with strips cut from the blue checked binding fabric.

Stars in Noord-Holland

BY AKKA PHILIPS

FINISHED SIZE: 48½" x 64½"
BLOCK SIZE: 8" x 8"

I made this quilt "between two houses." Our old house sold while the new one was still being built and we had no idea where to go. Luckily, a friend offered us her place to stay, for as long as needed. The only thing I could take with me were some of my favorite fabrics—traditional prints and some solids. I didn't have a special quilt in mind to work on, but making stars somehow made me feel happy. I ended up with thirty-five stars, all sewn by hand!

After we moved into our new home, I decided to put them together for a small wall hanging, intending to make it into a full-size bed quilt at a later date.

Materials: 44"-WIDE FABRIC

Assorted scraps of your favorite fabrics—flower prints, plaids, stripes, pin dots, and some vivid solids
⅝ yd. dark stripe for outer triangles in pieced border and binding
¼ yd. light stripe for inner triangles in pieced border
1⅞ yds. for backing
52" x 68" piece of batting

Cutting

Use the templates on pages 68–69 to cut enough pieces for 35 star blocks and the pieced borders.

From assorted scraps, cut for each block:
    1 Template A
    4 Template B
    4 Template C
    12 Template D

From the light stripe for the border, cut:
    48 Template D

From the dark stripe for the border, cut:
    56 Template D

From assorted solids and prints for the pieced border, cut:
    52 Template A

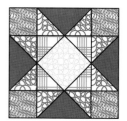

Star Block

Stars in Noord-Holland by Akka Philips, 1992, Meddelie, The Netherlands, 48½" x 64½".

Directions

Blocks

Assemble each block, following the steps below.
1. Arrange the pieces for each block in a pleasing arrangement.
2. Sew a Piece D to opposite sides of Piece A, then add Piece D to the remaining sides. Press the seams toward Piece A.

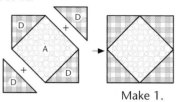

Make 1.

3. Sew 2 Piece D to each Piece C. Press the seams toward Piece C.

Make 4.

4. Sew the completed units and Piece B together in horizontal rows, pressing seams in the direction of the arrows. Join the rows to complete the block.

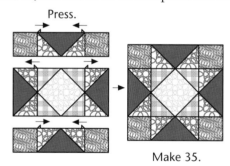

Make 35.

5. Lay out the completed blocks in a pleasing color arrangement, making 7 rows of 5 blocks each.
6. Sew the blocks together in horizontal rows, pressing the joining seams in opposite directions from row to row.

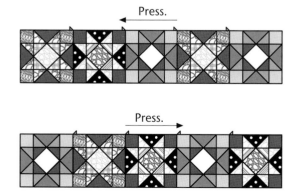

7. Join the rows to complete the quilt top.

Borders and Finishing

Refer to the general directions for quilt finishing, beginning on page 86.
1. Piece the borders, following the diagrams below.

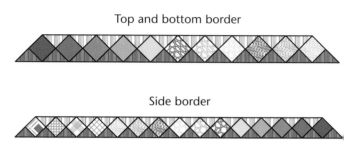

2. Sew the borders to the quilt, mitering the corners as shown on pages 84–85.
3. Layer the quilt top with batting and backing; baste.
4. Quilt as desired.
5. Bind the edges with strips cut from the remaining dark stripe.

Stars in Noord-Holland
Stars in Holland
Template A

straight of grain

1/4" seam allowance

68

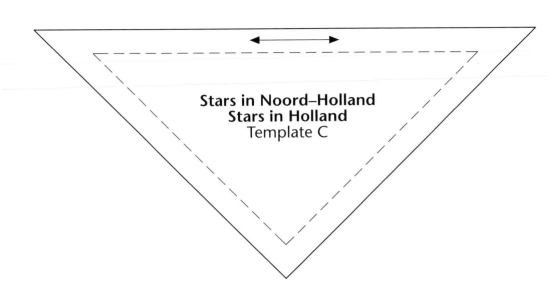

**Stars in Noord–Holland
Stars in Holland**
Template C

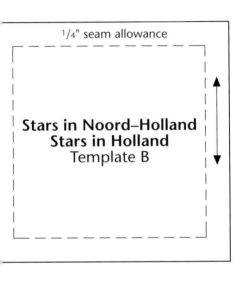

¹/₄" seam allowance

**Stars in Noord–Holland
Stars in Holland**
Template B

Stars in Noord–Holland
Template E

straight of grain

**Stars in Noord–Holland
Stars in Holland**
Template D

Stars in Holland

BY LIESBETH ERNST

FINISHED SIZE: 57½" x 81½"
BLOCK SIZE: 8" x 8"

Block 1   Block 2

Here's another colorful star quilt for you to stitch. It is made of two different blocks for added visual interest. Use fabrics from your scrap bag or buy a variety of color-coordinated fabrics to cut the pieces.

Materials: 44"-WIDE FABRIC

Assorted scraps in a variety of prints and solids (red, red-and-white, blue, and blue-and white)
⅓ yd. red solid for middle border
1⅛ yds. dark blue for outer border and binding
4¾ yds. for backing
62" x 85" piece of batting

Cutting

Use the templates on pages 68–69. Make 20 each of Block 1 and Block 2.

From assorted scraps, cut:

Block 1	Block 2	Pieced Inner Border
1 Template A	12 Template C	108 Template C
4 Template B	1 Template E	
4 Template C		
12 Template D		

From the red for middle border, cut:
　8 strips, each 1¾" wide, cutting across the width of the fabric.

From the dark blue for outer border, cut:
　8 strips, each 4¾" wide, cutting across the width of the fabric.

70

*Stars in Holland by Liesbeth Ernst, 1992, Amsterdam, The Netherlands, 57½" x 81½". Liesbeth's
red-white-and-blue stars sparkle in this scrappy quilt made from typical Dutch fabrics.
Photographed in the village of Marken.*

Directions

Blocks

1. Lay out the pieces for each Block 1 in a pleasing arrangement.
2. Assemble each block, following steps 2–4 on page 68. Make 20 of Block 1.
3. Lay out the pieces for each Block 2 in a pleasing arrangement. Sew each block together, following steps 4–6 below.
4. Sew a Piece C to opposite sides of Piece E, then sew a Piece C to each remaining side of E to create the center unit. Press seams toward E.

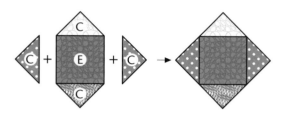

5. Sew the remaining C pieces together in pairs for the corner units. Press the seam toward the darker fabric in each pair.

Make 4.

6. Sew triangle units to opposite sides of the center unit, then to the 2 remaining sides. Press seams toward the center unit.

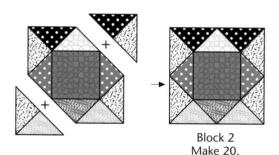

Block 2
Make 20.

Quilt Top Assembly

1. Arrange the blocks in 8 rows of 5 blocks each as shown in the quilt plan on page 70.
2. Sew blocks together in horizontal rows, pressing the seams in opposite directions from row to row.

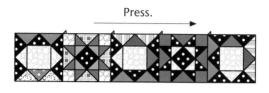

Press.

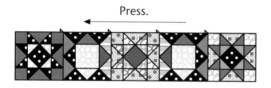

Press.

3. Sew the rows together.
4. For each side pieced inner border, join 32 triangles into pairs as shown. Join the triangle pairs, adding 1 more triangle to the end of the completed strip for a total of 33 triangles in each strip.

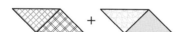

Join triangle pairs into pieced inner border strips.

For the top and bottom border, join 20 triangles into pairs. Join the triangle pairs, adding 1 more triangle to the end of the completed strip for a total of 21 triangles in each strip.

5. Sew the pieced borders to the quilt top, mitering the corners as shown on pages 84–85.
6. Stitch the border corners together, stitching from the corner to the outer edge.
7. For the top and bottom middle borders, cut 1 of the red middle border strips into 2 equal lengths. Sew 1 half strip to each remaining red border strip. Repeat with dark outer blue border strips. Sew the middle and outer border strips together in red/blue pairs.

Re◄
Blu

Make 2.

8. For each side border, sew 2 red middle border strips together to make a longer strip. Cut the remaining border strip into equal lengths. Sew 1 to the end of each red border strip. Repeat with the dark blue outer border strips. Sew the resulting middle and outer border strips together in red/blue pairs.
9. Measure the quilt top for mitered borders* as shown on page 84 and cut the border strips to the required lengths.
10. Sew the borders to the quilt top, mitering the corners as shown on pages 84–85.

* The quilt shown in the photo has mitered inner borders (red) and straight-cut outer borders (dark blue). You may apply borders in this manner if you prefer.

Quilt Finishing

Refer to the general directions for quilt finishing, beginning on page 86.
1. Layer the quilt top with batting and backing; baste.
2. Quilt as desired.
3. Bind the edges with strips cut from the remaining dark blue fabric.

Christmas Greeting Cards

BY WILLEMIEN MAK-AKKERMAN

*T*hese special greeting cards were made Log Cabin style on a paper foundation. They provide a wonderful way to use up small scraps. Place them behind the opening of a purchased blank card or one you make yourself. You can also use the completed blocks to make small ornaments.

Materials

Scraps of fabric, with small, dense prints and
    small motifs
Gold and silver fabric or ribbon
Red and green satin*
Plain paper
Pencil and ruler
Glue stick
Paper scissors
Rotary cutter, cutting mat, and ruler (optional)

*You may use bias binding if available.

Directions

Use the full-scale patterns on pages 76 and 77. The numbers on each refer to the sewing sequence for adding the strips.
Note: The pattern for the Offset Log Cabin block is shown in the following illustrations.

1. Trace the desired pattern onto plain paper, extending all lines as shown in the drawing next to it. Make the lines dark so they show through the fabric. If you wish, you may photocopy the pattern of your choice.

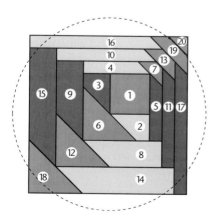

2. Cut fabric strips, using scissors or a rotary cutter. Rotary cutting gives better results. Cut strips ½" wider than the strip measurement on the pattern you are using. Some patterns require more than one strip width so be sure to measure first. Cut the pieces for the center slightly larger so a scant ¼" of fabric extends beyond all lines.

   Cut the strips that will be at the outer edge of the block 1" wide to allow room to stitch them to the outer edge of the paper foundation.

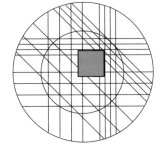

3. Use glue stick to hold Piece #1 in place on the paper foundation.

4. Position the strip for Piece #2 on top of the center piece with raw edges even. The strip should extend beyond the top and bottom lines of the area the strip will cover. Be particularly careful to cut those strips that will be crossed on the diagonal long enough. It's a good idea to position the strip on the foundation and, while holding it in place with one hand, use the other hand to flip it back onto the design to check to see that it is long enough.

   Stitch the strip in place. If you can use the edge of your presser foot as a guide for a ¼"-wide seam allowance, do so. Otherwise, you will have to "eye" the stitching by focusing on the line that extends beyond the ends of the strip you are adding. Carefully lower the needle into the fabric on the line and stitch slowly, aiming at the end of the line beyond the strip. There is no need to backstitch.

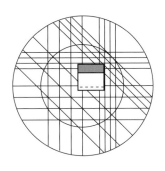

5. Trim the seam allowance to ⅛" and finger press the strip onto the paper foundation.

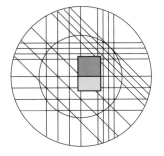

6. Add Piece #3 in the same manner.

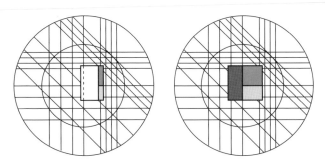

7. Continue adding strips in numerical order until the design is completed. Remember to cut the strips for the last round of pieces at least 1" wide.

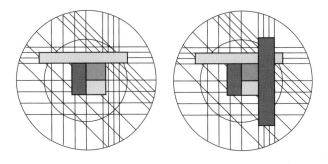

8. Stitch the outer edge of each of the last strips in the finished block to the paper foundation.

   Note: It is not necessary to remove the paper foundation.

9. Position the completed patchwork piece behind the opening in the card and glue in place. Cover the back of the patchwork with a piece of colored paper and glue in place. Set some heavy books on top and allow the glue to dry.

   Creative Option: Cut a backing fabric the same size as the finished patchwork and stitch it to the patchwork with right sides together, catching a loop of ribbon in the seam at the top. Leave an opening for turning. Turn right side out and press. Slipstitch the opening closed.

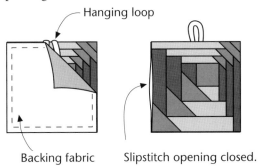

Hanging loop

Backing fabric   Slipstitch opening closed.

Offset Log Cabin

Pineapple

Tree #1

Tree #2

Offset Pineapple

St. Nicolaas Doll Cookie

SPECULAASPOP

Ingredients

3 cups flour
⅔ cup butter or margarine, softened
½ cup dark brown sugar
Pinch of baking powder
Pinch of salt
Milk to soften the dough
2 tsp. cinnamon
1 tsp. nutmeg
½ tsp. powdered cloves
Blanched almonds for decorating

1. Preheat the oven to 350° F.
2. Knead all ingredients into a soft ball.
3. To prepare the wooden mold*, dust it with flour.
4. Press the dough into the mold and cut away any excess dough so the surface is even.
5. Line a baking sheet with greased waxed paper. Carefully turn the mold onto the sheet.
6. Decorate the doll with almonds.
7. Place the baking sheet in the center of the oven and bake for 30–35 minutes.

*We make these cookies using a special wooden mold, but if one is not available, you can make the cookies without a mold.

1. Roll out the dough on a lightly floured surface to ⅛" thickness.
2. Cut with a cookie cutter or roll the dough into balls. Flatten the cookie balls with the floured tines of a fork.

*I*n the Netherlands, December is the month of family traditions. Families and friends come together for Christmas and New Year's Day. December festivities begin with the celebration of the birthday (5 December) of Sint Nicolaas (not to be confused with Santa Claus).

Sint Nicolaas is the patron of girls who want to marry, and so of all amorous people. When it comes to gift giving on the fifth of December, it is obvious that you want to give part of yourself to your lover. Of course, this is not possible. Instead, you can offer an image of yourself as a doll—a doll made of speculaas; a kind of hard, brown spicy cookie. By offering this vrijer (suitor) you say, I love you! This cookie is very popular and we continue to eat speculaasjes, a smaller version, after Sint Nicolaas's birthday.

General Directions

Included in this chapter are the basic quiltmaking techniques you need to know to assemble and finish the quilts featured in this book.

Fabric Selection for Patchwork and Appliqué

Select high-quality, 100% cotton fabrics. They hold their shape well and are easy to handle. Cotton blends can be more difficult to stitch and press. Yardage requirements for all the projects in this book are based on 42 usable inches of fabric after pre-shrinking. With careful cutting, you may have some fabric left over to add to your fabric collection.

Several of the quilts in this book call for a large assortment of scraps rather than give exact yardage requirements. Dutch quilters are, by nature, quite frugal, and often make scrappy quilts to use pieces left over from other projects. If you have access to scraps, feel free to use them, and purchase only those fabrics you need to complete the color selection for the quilt plan you are following. If you do not have a wide assortment of scraps, you may wish to purchase fat quarters (18" x 22" pieces often available in quilt shops). Trading with other quilters is another nice way to expand your collection for scrap quilts. Consider sharing fat quarters by cutting them in half (9" x 22") for even more variety. If you prefer a more planned approach, make sample blocks in your desired color/fabric combinations and calculate the required yardage for your version of the scrap quilt.

Preshrink all fabric to test for colorfastness and to remove excess dye. Wash dark and light colors separately so that dark colors do not run onto light fabrics. Some fabrics may require several rinses to eliminate the excess dyes. Iron fabrics so that the pieces will be accurate when they are cut.

Quiltmaking Supplies

Sewing machine: You need a machine in good working order for machine piecing.

Walking foot or darning foot: This attachment is useful for machine quilting.

Scissors: Use your best scissors to cut fabric only. Use an older pair of scissors to cut paper, cardboard, and template plastic. Small, 4"-long scissors with sharp points are handy for clipping thread.

Rotary cutting equipment (optional): If you wish to rotary cut the pieces for your quilt, you will need a rotary cutter, cutting mat, and a clear acrylic ruler. Two handy sizes include a 6" x 24" ruler and a 6" square.

Thread: Use a good-quality, all-purpose cotton or cotton-covered polyester thread. For machine piecing, select a light neutral color, such as beige or tan for light-colored fabrics, and a dark neutral, such as dark gray for darker fabrics.

Thread for appliqué should match the color of the appliqué pieces rather than the background fabric. If it is not possible to match the exact color, choose thread that is slightly darker than the fabric. If the appliqué fabric contains many different colors, choose a neutral-colored thread that blends with the predominant color in the fabric.

Use quilting thread only for the quilting process. It is thicker than all-purpose thread and may show if used for piecing or appliqué.

Needles: For machine piecing, a fine needle (10/70) works well for most lightweight cottons. For heavier fabrics, use size 12/80.

When choosing a needle for appliqué, the most important consideration is the size of the needle. A fine needle will glide easily through the edges of the appliqué pieces. Size 10 (fine) to size 12 (very fine) needles work well.

Pins: Long, fine "quilters' pins" with glass or plastic heads are easy to handle.

Template plastic: Use clear or frosted plastic to make durable, accurate templates. This plastic is available at quilt shops.

Seam ripper: You will need this handy tool to remove stitches from incorrectly sewn seams.

Marking tools: A variety of tools is available to mark fabrics when tracing around templates or when marking quilting lines. You can mark fabric with a regular pencil or fine-lead mechanical pencil. Use a silver or yellow marking pencil on darker fabrics. Chalk pencils or chalk-wheel markers also make clear marks on fabric. Be sure to test whatever tool you decide to use on your fabric first to make sure you can remove the marks easily without damaging the fabric.

Patchwork Techniques

Most of the quilts in this book require templates. Full-size templates are included with the quilt plans or on the large pullout pattern sheets in the back of this book. If you prefer to rotary cut and have experience with rotary-cutting techniques, you will find it easy to rotary cut many of the shapes required. For detailed information on rotary cutting, you might wish to consult *Shortcuts: A Concise Guide to Rotary Cutting* by Donna Lynn Thomas.

Making and Using Templates

All templates include the required ¼"-wide seam allowances. They are also marked with a grain-line arrow for correct placement on your fabric. Many Dutch quilters prefer to piece by hand in the traditional manner, while others are adopting speedier machine-piecing techniques. Make your templates, using the appropriate method for your preferred method of piecing.

Templates for Machine Piecing

1. Trace the templates for the quilt you are making onto template plastic. Trace around the outer edge of the template along the cutting line. Mark the grain-line arrow and the name of the quilt on each template. It is not necessary to mark the seam lines. For some quilts, you may be directed to mark seam-line intersections for matching purposes.

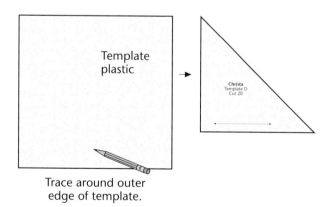

Trace around outer edge of template.

2. Carefully cut out each template on the marked line. Accuracy is important.
3. Place the template face down on the wrong side of the fabric, aligning the grain-line arrow with the straight grain of the fabric. Trace around it with a sharp pencil.

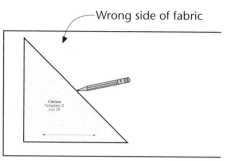

Trace onto fabric.

4. Cut the shape from the fabric on the traced line, using scissors or rotary-cutting tools.
5. Be sure to use an accurate ¼"-wide seam allowance to stitch the pieces together. See below.

Tip: For some quilts, it is necessary to mark the seam intersections for matching purposes. To do this, use the point of a large darning needle to pierce the template plastic at the intersections. It is easier to do this if you warm the point of the needle in the flame of a candle first. Using a sharp pencil, mark the seam-line intersections on each piece through the holes you made in the template.

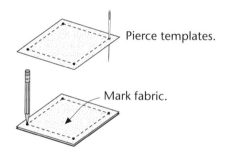

Pierce templates.

Mark fabric.

Templates for Hand Piecing

Unlike templates for machine piecing, templates for hand piecing do not include seam allowances.

1. Trace the templates you need onto template plastic, tracing on the dashed seam line rather than the cutting line. Mark the grain-line arrow and the name of the quilt on each template for future reference.

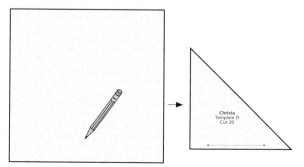

Trace on dashed seam line.

2. Place the template face down on the wrong side of the fabric, aligning the grain-line arrow with the straight grain of the fabric. Use a sharp pencil to trace around the template. The marked line is the stitching line. If you need to trace several of the same template onto the fabric, be sure to leave at least ½" of fabric between the marked pieces for seam allowances.

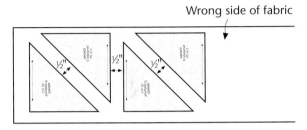

Wrong side of fabric

3. Add ¼"-wide seam allowances all around each traced shape. Use a ruler and a sharp pencil. Carefully cut out the templates on the outer line.

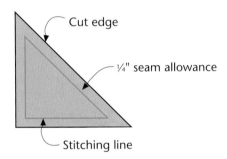

Cut edge

¼" seam allowance

Stitching line

Piecing

The most important thing to remember about piecing is to maintain a consistent ¼"-wide seam allowance. Otherwise, the quilt block will not be the desired finished size. If that happens, the size of everything else in the quilt is affected. Measurements for all components of each quilt are based on blocks that finish accurately to the desired size plus ¼" on each edge for seam allowances.

Before you begin to assemble your quilt blocks, it is a good idea to lay out the pieces for each block, following the block diagram given with each quilt. Then assemble each block, following the piecing diagrams and using either machine- or hand-piecing techniques.

Machine Piecing

The pieces you cut for machine piecing do not have marked seam lines if you used the template method for machine piecing described above. Therefore, it is extremely important to mark an accurate stitching guide first. Some machines have a special quilting foot designed so that the right-hand and left-hand edges of the foot measure exactly ¼" from the center needle position. This feature allows you to use the edge of the presser foot to guide the edge of the fabric for a perfect ¼"-wide seam allowance.

If your machine doesn't have such a foot, you can create a seam guide so it will be easy to stitch an accurate ¼"-wide seam allowance.

To mark an accurate seam guide, follow these steps:
1. Place a ruler or piece of graph paper with four squares to the inch under your presser foot.
2. Gently lower the needle onto the first ¼" line from the right edge of the ruler or paper. Place several layers of masking tape along the right-hand edge of the ruler or paper, being careful that it does not interfere with the feed dog. Test your new guide to make sure your seams are ¼" wide; if not, readjust your guide.

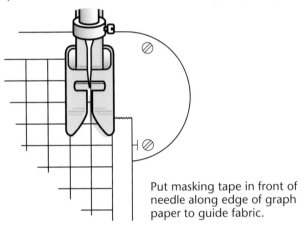

Put masking tape in front of needle along edge of graph paper to guide fabric.

When sewing the pieces together by machine, make sure the raw edges match and guide them along the edge of your seam guide. To make machine piecing go faster, try chain piecing. It saves time and thread.

1. Start by sewing the first pair of pieces. Sew from cut edge to cut edge, using 12–15 stitches per inch. At the end of the seam, stop sewing, but do not cut the thread.
2. Feed the next pair of pieces under the presser foot, as close as possible to the first pair.
3. Continue feeding pieces through the machine without cutting the threads in between. There is no need to backstitch, since each seam will be crossed and held in place by another seam as you complete the blocks and sew them together.
4. Remove the chain from the machine and clip the threads between the pieces.

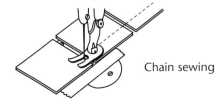

Chain sewing

Hand Piecing

1. Place the pieces right sides together, matching the seam lines. If you cut and marked the pieces accurately, the seam lines should align and the raw edges should match. However, if they do not, concentrate on matching the stitching lines.

2. Place a pin through one corner at the seam-line intersection of the piece on top and pierce the piece on the bottom at the matching seam-line intersection. Repeat at the opposite end of the pieces. Use additional pins to keep seam lines matched for stitching.

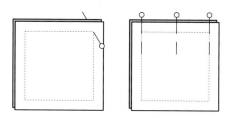

3. Thread a hand sewing needle with an 18" length of sewing thread and knot one end.

4. Insert the needle at the seam-line intersection, not at the cut edge of the pieces. Take a backstitch in the same spot.

5. Load the needle with several small stitches, making sure all stitches are on the marked seam line. Complete the stitches and continue in the same manner until you reach the seam intersection at the other end of the seam line.

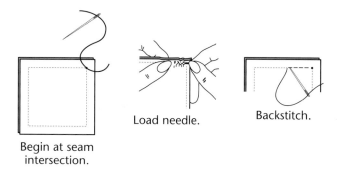

Begin at seam intersection.

Load needle.

Backstitch.

6. Backstitch to secure.

Tip: When seams within the block you are making intersect each other, hand stitch the seam without catching the crossing seam allowances in the stitching. Instead, make a small backstitch on each side of the seam-allowance intersection to hold it securely. This makes it easier to accurately match seam lines.

Pressing

The traditional rule in quiltmaking is to press seams to one side, toward the darker color whenever possible. Press the seam flat as stitched, first from the wrong side, then press the seam in the desired direction from the right side. Press carefully to avoid distorting the shapes.

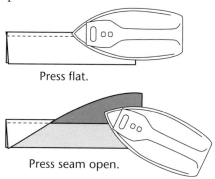

Press flat.

Press seam open.

When joining two seamed units, it is usually possible to plan ahead and press the seam allowances in opposite directions as shown. This reduces bulk and makes it easier to match seam lines. Where two seams meet, the seam allowances will butt up against each other, making it easier to join units with perfectly matched seam intersections.

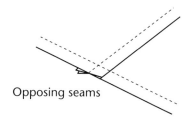

Opposing seams

Appliqué

The appliquéd quilts featured in this book were made using the freezer-paper method of appliqué. Directions for this method follow. Substitute another method if you prefer.

Freezer-Paper Appliqué

Use freezer paper (plastic coated on one side) to help make perfectly shaped appliqués. You can trace around a template or simply trace the design onto the freezer paper, directly from the page in the book or the pullout pattern sheet at the back of this book.

1. Place the freezer paper, plastic side down, on top of the pattern and trace the design with a sharp pencil.

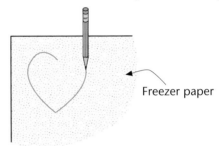

Freezer paper

2. Cut out the freezer-paper design on the pencil line. Do not add seam allowances.
3. With the plastic-coated side against the wrong side of the fabric, iron the freezer paper in place, using a hot, dry iron.

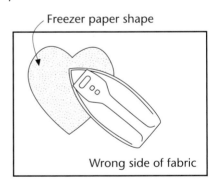

Freezer paper shape

Wrong side of fabric

4. Cut out the shape, adding ¼"-wide seam allowances around the outside edge of the freezer paper.

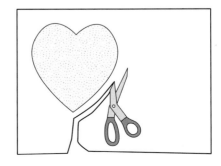

5. Turn and baste the seam allowance over the freezer-paper edges by hand or use a glue stick. (Clip inside points and fold outside points.)

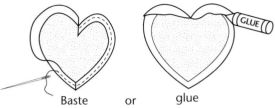

Baste   or   glue

6. Pin or baste the design to the background fabric. Appliqué the design using the Traditional Appliqué Stitch (below).
7. After the design has been appliquéd, remove any basting stitches. Cut a small slit in the background fabric behind the appliqué and remove the freezer paper with tweezers. If you used a glue stick, soak the piece in warm water for a few minutes before removing the freezer paper.

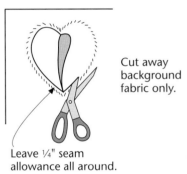

Cut away background fabric only.

Leave ¼" seam allowance all around.

The Traditional Appliqué Stitch

The traditional appliqué stitch or blind stitch is appropriate for sewing all appliqué shapes, including sharp points and curves.

1. Tie a knot in a single strand of thread that is approximately 18" long.
2. Hide the knot by slipping the needle into the seam allowance from the wrong side of the appliqué piece, bringing it out on the fold line.
3. Work from right to left if you are right-handed, or left to right if you are left-handed.
4. Start the first stitch by moving the needle straight off the appliqué, inserting the needle into the background fabric. Let the needle travel under the background fabric, parallel to the edge of the appliqué, bringing it up about ⅛" away, along the pattern line.
5. As you bring the needle up, pierce the edge of the appliqué piece, catching only one or two threads of the folded edge.
6. Move the needle straight off the appliqué into the background fabric. Let your needle travel under the background, bringing it up about ⅛" away, again catching the edge of the appliqué.
7. Give the thread a slight tug and continue stitching.

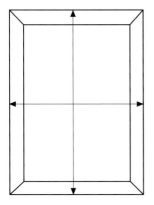

Wrong side

8. To end your stitching, pull the needle through to the wrong side. Behind the appliqué piece, take two small stitches, making knots by taking your needle through the loops. Check the right side to see if the thread will shadow through your background when finished. If it does, take one more small stitch through the back side to direct the tail of the thread under the appliqué fabric.

Borders

After making the required blocks and assembling the quilt top, you are ready to add borders. The first step is to measure the completed quilt top. The edges of a quilt often measure slightly longer than the distance through the quilt center, due to stretching or stitching inaccuracies that occur while you are making the blocks and assembling the quilt top. Sometimes, each edge is a different length. If you measure the quilt top through the center in both directions to determine how long to cut the border strips, the finished quilt will be as straight and as "square" as possible, without wavy edges.

Plain border strips are commonly cut along the crosswise grain and sewn together when extra length is required to fit the quilt. Borders cut from the lengthwise grain of the fabric require extra yardage, but seaming the required length is not necessary.

Most of the quilt borders in this book have mitered corners, but directions for straight-cut borders are also included here.

Borders with Mitered Corners

1. First estimate the finished outside dimensions of your quilt, including borders. Add at least ½" for seam allowances. It is safer, however, to add 2" to 3" to give yourself some leeway. Cut border strips to match these lengths. (Cutting dimensions for the borders in this book are based on allowing for this extra length. If you are short on fabric, or very frugal, you may want to adjust these lengths.)

   For example, if your quilt top measures 35½" x 50½" across the center and you want a 5"-wide finished border, your quilt will measure 45" x 60" after the borders are attached. You would cut the border strips 48" and 63" long.

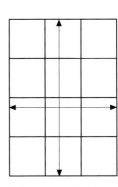

Estimate outside dimensions, including borders.

2. Fold the quilt in half and mark the centers of the quilt edges. Fold each border strip in half and mark each center with a pin.

3. Measure the length and width of the quilt across the center. Note the measurements.

4. Place a pin at each end of the side border strips to mark the length of the quilt top. Repeat with the top and bottom borders.

Measure quilt top without borders.

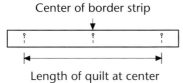

Center of border strip

Length of quilt at center

5. Pin the borders to the quilt top, matching the centers. Line up the pins at either end of the border strip with the edges of the quilt. Stitch, beginning and ending the stitching ¼" from the raw edges of the quilt top. Repeat with the remaining borders.

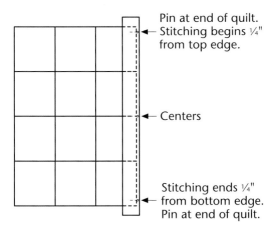

Pin at end of quilt.
Stitching begins ¼" from top edge.

Centers

Stitching ends ¼" from bottom edge.
Pin at end of quilt.

6. Lay the first corner to be mitered on the ironing board. Fold under one border strip at a 45° angle and adjust so seam lines match perfectly. Press and pin the mitered seam.

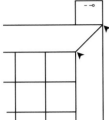

7. Fold the quilt with right sides together, lining up the edges of the border. If necessary, use a ruler to draw a pencil line on the crease to make the line more visible. Stitch on the pressed crease, sewing from the corner to the outside edge.

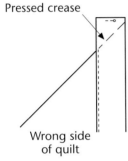

Pressed crease

Wrong side of quilt

8. Press the seam open and trim away excess border strips, leaving a ¼"-wide seam allowance.
9. Repeat with remaining corners.

Borders with Straight-Cut Corners

1. Measure the length of the quilt top through the center. Cut border strips to that measurement, piecing as necessary; mark the centers of the quilt top and the border strips. Pin the borders to the sides of the quilt top, matching the center marks and ends and easing as necessary. Sew the border strips in place. Press the seams toward the border.

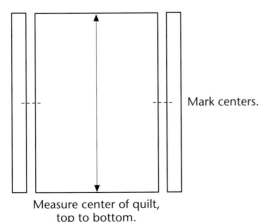

Mark centers.

Measure center of quilt, top to bottom.

2. Measure the width of the quilt through the center, including the side borders just added. Cut border strips to that measurement, piecing as necessary; mark the center of the quilt top and the border strips. Pin the borders to the sides of the quilt top, matching the center marks and ends and easing as necessary. Sew the border strips in place. Press the seams toward the border.

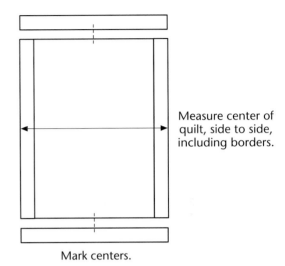

Measure center of quilt, side to side, including borders.

Mark centers.

Note: The above directions assume that you will add the side borders first, then the top and bottom borders, but the borders on some quilts in this book were added to the top and bottom first. In this case, you would measure the width first, attach the top and bottom borders, and then measure the length with the borders included, to cut and add the side border strips.

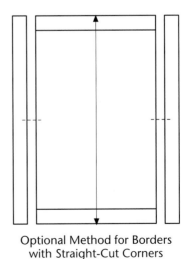

Optional Method for Borders with Straight-Cut Corners

Quilt Finishing

Marking the Quilting Lines

Whether or not to mark the quilting designs depends upon the type of quilting you will be doing. Marking is not necessary if you plan to quilt in-the-ditch or outline quilt a uniform distance from seam lines. Mark complex quilting designs on the quilt top before the quilt is layered with batting and backing.

Choose a marking tool that will be visible on your fabric and test it on fabric scraps to be sure the marks can be removed easily. See "Marking Tools" on page 79 for options. Masking tape can also be used to mark straight quilting. Tape only small sections at a time and remove the tape when you stop at the end of the day; otherwise the sticky residue may be difficult to remove from the fabric.

Layering the Quilt Sandwich

Once your quilt top is marked for quilting, you are ready to assemble the layers in the quilt sandwich—quilt top, batting, and backing.

1. Cut the quilt backing at least 2"–4" larger than the quilt top all the way around. For large quilts, it is usually necessary to sew two or three lengths of fabric together to make a backing of the required size. Press the backing seams open to make quilting easier.

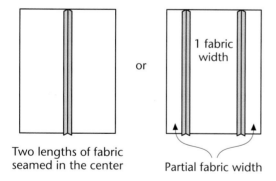

Two lengths of fabric seamed in the center

or

1 fabric width

Partial fabric width

2. Spread the backing, wrong side up, on a flat, clean surface. Anchor it with pins or masking tape. Be careful not to stretch the backing out of shape.
3. Cut the batting the same size as the backing. Spread the batting over the backing, smoothing out any wrinkles.
4. Place the quilt top on top of the batting. Smooth out any wrinkles and make sure the edges of the quilt top are parallel to the edges of the backing.
5. Baste with needle and thread, starting in the center and working diagonally to each corner. Continue basting in a grid of horizontal and vertical lines 6"–8" apart. Finish by basting around the edges.

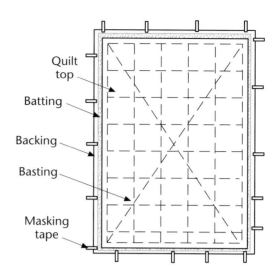

Quilt top
Batting
Backing
Basting
Masking tape

Note: For machine quilting, you may baste the layers with #2 rustproof safety pins. Place pins about 6"–8" apart, away from the area you intend to quilt.

6. Quilt as desired by hand or machine.

Quilting

The quilts in this book were hand quilted, but you may machine quilt if you prefer. Quilting in-the-ditch and outline quilting ¼" away from the seam lines are appropriate choices for the featured patterns, but feel free to add more elaborate quilting patterns if desired.

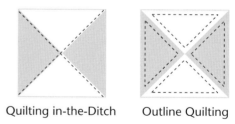

Quilting in-the-Ditch   Outline Quilting

Binding

Bindings can be made from straight-cut or bias-cut strips of fabric. Many of the quilts in this book were made with single-layer binding strips that finish to ¼" wide. If you prefer a wider binding or a double-layer binding, you may need additional fabric. For single-layer binding that finishes to ¼", cut the strips 1⅛" wide. The extra ⅛" allows enough room to wrap the binding over the thickness of the batting. For double-layer binding, cut the strips 2½" wide. For bindings wider than ¼" finished, adjust the binding strip width as needed.

To cut straight-grain binding strips:
   Cut strips of the desired width across the width of the fabric. You will need enough strips to go around the perimeter of the quilt plus 10" for seams and the corners in a mitered fold.

To cut bias-grain binding strips:
1. Fold a square of fabric on the diagonal.

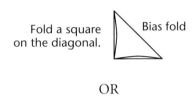

Fold a square on the diagonal.   Bias fold

OR

Fold a ½-yard piece as shown in the diagrams below, paying careful attention to the location of the lettered corners.

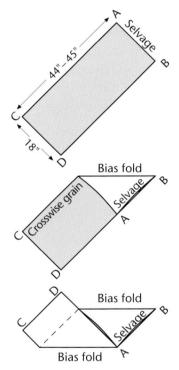

2. Cut strips of the desired width, using a rotary cutter and ruler and cutting perpendicular to the folds as shown. If you are using scissors, measure and mark the cutting lines on the folded fabric first, then cut on the marked lines.

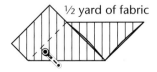

½ yard of fabric

Bias fold
Square of fabric

To attach single-layer binding:
1. Trim the batting and backing even with the quilt-top edges.
2. Sew strips, right sides together, to make one long piece of binding. Press seams open.

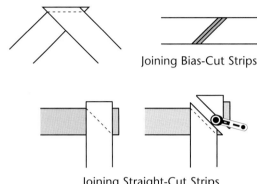

Joining Bias-Cut Strips

Joining Straight-Cut Strips

3. Turn under ¼" at a 45° angle at one end of the strip and press. Turning the end under at an angle distributes the bulk so you won't have a lump where the two ends of the binding meet.

4. Starting on one side of the quilt, stitch the binding to the quilt, keeping the raw edges even with the quilt-top edge and using a ¼"-wide seam allowance. End the stitching ¼" from the corner of the quilt and backstitch. Clip the thread.

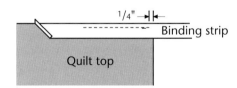

1/4"
Binding strip
Quilt top

5. Turn the quilt so that you will be stitching down the next side. Fold the binding up away from the quilt.

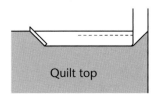

Quilt top

6. Fold binding back down onto itself, parallel with the edge of the quilt top. Begin stitching at the edge, backstitching to secure.

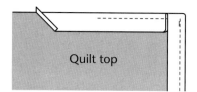

7. Repeat on the remaining edges and corners of the quilt. When you reach the beginning of the binding, overlap the beginning stitches by about 1" and cut away any excess binding, trimming the end at a 45° angle.

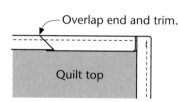

8. Fold the binding over the raw edges of the quilt to the back and turn the raw edge under. Blindstitch in place with the folded edge just covering the row of machine stitching. A miter will form at each corner. Blindstitch the mitered corners in place.

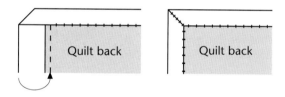

To attach double-layer binding:

1. Trim the batting and backing even with the quilt-top edges.
2. Sew the binding strips together, making one long piece of binding as shown in step 2 for single-layer binding.
3. Fold the binding strip in half lengthwise, wrong sides together, and press.
4. Open the strip and turn under ¼" at a 45° angle at one end of the strip. Press. Fold in half again.

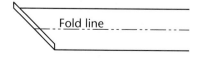

5. With both raw edges of the binding strip even with the raw edge of the quilt top, stitch the binding to the quilt, following steps 4–7 for single-layer binding. Tuck the end of the binding into the fold and finish the seam.

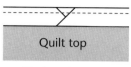

6. Complete the binding as shown in the illustrations under step 8 for single-layer binding.

Making a Label

Be sure to sign and date your quilt. Future generations will be interested to know more than just who made it and when. Labels can be as elaborate or as simple as you wish. Embroider, type, or write the desired information, including the name of the quilt, your name, your city and state, the date, the name of the recipient if it is a gift, and any other interesting or important information about the quilt.